M1

YORK *The Continuing City*

YORK *The Continuing City*

Patrick Nuttgens

FABER AND FABER LIMITED · LONDON

First published in 1976
by Faber and Faber Limited
3 Queen Square, London WC1
Printed in Great Britain by
W & J Mackay Limited
Chatham

ISBN 0 571 09733 2

To the members of York Georgian Society
and York Civic Trust, York's architects,
and the many hundreds of York's citizens
who have listened to my lectures about the city,
this book is gratefully dedicated

'The history of York falls somewhat short of being a complete epitome of English history; but it is almost a complete index to it.'
Charles Brunton Knight, *A History of the City of York*, 1944

Contents

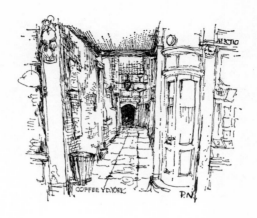

List of maps   *page* 10

List of plates   11

Introduction: The Genesis of this Book   13

1   The Legionary Fortress   19

2   The Market   27

3   Motte and Minster   40

4   The King's Manor   59

5   The Assembly Rooms   67

6   Railway Street   84

7   The Precinct   101

    Bibliographical Note   117

    Index   121

Maps

between pages 116 and 117

1   Roman York
2   Anglo-Danish York
3   Mediaeval York
4   Georgian York
5   Nineteenth-Century York
6   Modern York

*Acknowledgement is made to the City of York
for the use of the base map*

10

Plates

between pages 48 and 49

1   Mediaeval York, with Motte and Minster
2   Petergate: the Via Principalis of Roman York
3   Stonegate: the Via Praetoria of Roman York
4   All Saints, North Street: the type of a mediaeval church
5   The Minster in its immediate setting
6   The Ascension: ceiling boss in the Minster nave
7   The West Front of the Minster
8   Roman York, with wall and Multangular Tower
9   The Minster: Choir after restoration
10 The Minster: looking up the Central Tower
11 All Saints, Pavement: the 15th century lantern
12 The Defences: 13th century city wall enclosing the Minster
13 The Castle: Clifford's Tower on its motte
14 The oldest houses in York: Lady Row, Goodramgate
15 Walmgate Bar: 14th century gate and barbican
16 The Merchant Adventurers' Hall
17 Lady Peckitt's Yard
18 The King's Manor: home of the Council in the North
19 The King's Manor: University of York
20 The Treasurer's House
21 Coffee Yard, between Stonegate and Swinegate
22 Shambles: the butchers' street
23 Shambles: from butchers to books
24 Tower Place: Regency elegance
25 The Debtors' Prison, once the finest gaol in Europe, now the Castle Museum

Plates

26 Ouse Bridge Inn, on King's Staith

27 The Assembly Rooms, social centre of Georgian York

28 Cumberland House, on the riverside

29 The Judges' Lodging, Lendal

30 Bishopthorpe Palace, the home of the archbishops of York

31 The Mansion House

32 The Railway Station

33 The Yorkshire Museum

34 Lendal Bridge

35 St Leonard's Place: Regency houses now Council offices

36 Prospect Place: 19th century workers' houses

37 Scarcroft School

38 University of York: the lake and colleges

39 University of York: staff houses at Bleachfield

40 New Earswick: the garden village

Acknowledgement is made to the following for the photographs: the Shepherd Building Group Ltd. for plates 5, 6, 7, 9 and 10; the remainder of the photographs were taken by Keith Gibson

Introduction — The Genesis of this Book

In January 1962 I clambered out of a train at York Station and walked into the city to take up a new post. I was one of the little group of academics and administrators gathering in York for the setting up of a new university, the first messengers of what was rapidly to become a significant academic community. My own role in the foundation of that university was a junior one; I was primarily in York to take over the directorship of the Institute of Advanced Architectural Studies, one of the two graduate institutes that formed the nucleus of the new university. Inevitably, as the only architect on the academic staff for some years, I became closely involved in its development. It was an endlessly fascinating experience.

Looking back on that first winter and the academic year before any students arrived, I am still moved by the memory of a rare privilege and a great adventure. I suppose the people who join in that kind of experiment and throw in their lot with an uncertain future are essentially adventurers, in the truest sense of the term. My colleagues in those early months were lively, argumentative, often hilarious and always stimulating. Under the firm leadership of the first Vice Chancellor, Lord James of Rusholme, clear-headed, critical, witty and sometimes scathing, we spent long weekends arguing, driving out into the hills, eating and drinking, talking all the time, trying to come closer to an understanding of what a new university should be.

But most of the time I was working in the Institute, housed in the mediaeval church of St John, Ousebridge, brilliantly and colourfully restored by my predecessor Dr Singleton to provide a lecture hall in the nave, a small but superb library in the north aisle and offices in the south aisle. It was impeccably maintained and full of life and interest. A peal of bells still hung in the tower and bell-ringers came along from time to time to practise change-ringing and disturb the outside world. Later we moved the Institute to the King's

Manor, also in the middle of the city. As Chapter 4 indicates, it was an even more fascinating historic building, also brilliantly restored, this time by Bernard Feilden. It broke in upon me more and more that, without even trying, I was literally immersed in York's architectural history. I could not avoid looking at it wherever I turned. Nor could I avoid thinking about it as we discussed the formation of a university that was without question the most significant development in the social, economic and cultural life of the city for at least a century. For good or ill we were involved in the living history of a city and therefore we ought to know something about it. One of the results is this book.

I had in fact been in York before on three occasions. On one of them, travelling across the North of England with my father, fixing some of his stained glass windows into churches, we had stopped in York and looked at the mediaeval windows in All Saints North Street. It was not only the windows that were remarkable. All Saints North Street was at that time in the care of the Revd. Patrick Shaw, a man of high-church leanings, unstinting charity and positive ideas who filled the church with an abundant variety of church furniture and fittings and installed an anchorite in a concrete hermitage against the west gable, from which he could look through a small window into the church. For the first time I thought I knew what a mediaeval church must have looked—and smelled—like.

On another occasion, while preparing some lectures on Georgian architecture, I visited York to see its Georgian buildings and was shown round by the indefatigable Miss Pressly, who had retired from school teaching and founded the York Georgian Society, building it up into a constituent part of the city's life. That visit put me in touch with another section of York. I was given lunch at Terry's restaurant and stayed in the garden village of New Earswick.

Finally, I had attended a Summer School at the Institute and spent much of the time exploring York. The Secretary of the Institute, John West-Taylor, now the Registrar of the University, took me to two places which became fixed in my mind as symbols of York. The first was the Bay Horse in Blossom Street, now sensitively modernized in keeping with its old character, then an astonishing jumble of small timbered rooms with glazed panels, irregularly arranged around a tap room into whose gloom and crowded interior you peered through hatches and extricated your beer across a lead counter. The floors sloped down so that you entered at a run; there were Victorian iron tables and ceilings of a rich brown plaster, coloured by at least seventy years of tobacco smoke from innumerable pipes. The second was the marshalling yard behind York Station, where, in those days, steam engines lay heavily at night, like huge tired monsters, the fire and smoke from their mouths throwing an eerie glow across the gloom of the sidings, flickering across lines and wires and glittering on the windows of grey houses against the black sky.

I thought then—and still think now—that those institutions—the churches, the public houses, the railways and the learned societies—were basic constituents of the character of York. The sheer fascination of the city began to take hold of me. In the colder months, which was most of the year, I walked with a colleague to different pubs for lunch and so began to explore every road, lane and alley inside the walls. On sunnier days, when we were preparing for courses and not running one, I sometimes closed the Institute for a few hours and took the secretaries out in a boat for a picnic, rowing along the Ouse, slipping down the river between steep banks and warehouses, beneath bridges and a few cranes, wallowing—metaphorically—in the atmosphere of a great town. I was getting more and more obsessed with an urban phenomenon.

For York seemed to have everything that a city ought to have, except possibly two things: it was not sufficiently cosmopolitan and it was not, with a population of 100,000, very big. The first shortage was to some extent made up by the members of the university, including myself. The second I came to see, not as a disadvantage, but as a positive boon. The experience of the transformation of our towns and cities in the last fifteen years has persuaded many people that there must be a limit to the tolerable size of an urban community. I am increasingly convinced that the size of York is about right—just big enough to require investigation and provide surprises, just small enough to recognize many faces in the street, know most of the personalities and take part in the critical analysis and self-development of the city.

It was partly because of this conviction that I became involved in serious controversy about the future of the city. Distressed by the number of faceless new buildings appearing in the streets, many of them designed by York architects as well as by outsiders, I provoked a public row about the design of new buildings and the accelerating destruction of the city. To my surprise and temporary embarrassment, the argument attracted the attention of the national as well as the local press and made York the centre of a storm. It was a conflict between history and development and at the time development seemed to be winning without a protest. The climate has now changed and the idea of 'conservation'—nationally as well as locally—has become fashionable. The crisis in York was one of the stages in that change.

The controversy also illuminated for me something of the characteristic attitude of York's citizens. The people of York are not, on the whole, renowned for their sense of humour. York does not, like the cities of the Industrial North, spawn comedians; it does not even take readily to jokes. At least twice I have written what I foolishly imagined to be funny or satirical pieces about York and have been bitterly attacked, once even in a leader in the *Yorkshire Evening Press*. But the grim solemnity lies, actually very thinly, over a deeper seriousness and concern that occasionally expresses itself in quiet witticisms and sudden shafts of disarming sincerity. Perhaps in some way the Quaker influence in York has had something to do with this. I became aware of a very profound concern and a real, not uncritical, pride. Throughout the arguments, for all the toughness of language and the violence of opinions, I made many friends and very few enemies.

My own concern was not just with history or the preservation of the past; it was with the developing nature of the city, with its vital and coherent future as well as its historic past. I believed that the two sides could be brought together. So, after much discussion, did the councillors and officials of the city. There are now many new faces among them— of people dedicated to the continuity of the city and its change as well as its preservation. Inevitably some of the academics who had come to bring a new dimension to the old city became, as academics usually do, more conservative and resistant to change than the people who were there before. Like the commuters who move into an attractive village and found an amenity society to preserve the place and keep other people out, academics inevitably tend to make a corner for themselves and hope that no new winds will disturb the groves.

To some extent one of the early disappointments of the new university was its failure to inform and enrich the city's own cultural life. Only in one area—music—have the two nations come closely together. And that may be because, unusually for a university, its Music Department is committed to making music and not just talking about it to its own members. The essential condition for meaningful collaboration and unity between a city and a university is engagement in practical activity, not just in words.

The words in this book require some explanation. Although I left York five years ago to work in the new Polytechnic at Leeds I am still closely involved in York, chairman of the York Georgian Society and a member of the Council of York Civic Trust. Almost continu- ally for the last twelve years I have been reading about York, talking, lecturing and writing articles about it, taking visitors around it. I have attended more lectures than I can count, met most of its scholars and continued to explore the city itself. That has a bearing on this book. I must have missed something, but as far as I can tell I have been in every street in York and have looked at the outside (at least) of every house. I have rowed up and down the Ouse, walked along the Foss, made many a circuit of the walls, tried out (I believe) all the cafes, visited (I confess) nearly all the pubs. The result, as readers of this book will recognize, is that my knowledge of York, which is extensive and multifarious, is not all scholarly, is not just the product of dry research and does not all come from books.

Symptomatic of that is the fact that this book has no footnotes, the very signature of the academic. It has a selective bibliography, composed of items I have myself read, many of which I have also acquired. It does not list the many pictures I have worked through in the City Art Gallery, the many plans and prints I have looked at in the City Library, the many lessons I have learned from local people. Members of the York office of the Royal Commission on Historical Monuments have, for example, been stumping the town and occupying its lecture platforms for years. I cannot remember how many of their lectures

I have heard, how many conversations I have had, how much I have picked their brains. Between them and more recent archaeological studies, at the Minster and by the York Archaeological Trust, the underlying story of York is being rapidly revealed. This book is, I hope, a personal contribution.

If so, it is a contribution of a deliberate kind. It is concerned not so much with detail as with the discovery of the city as a whole. Many scholars know more than I shall ever know about special aspects and special periods; many investigators have explored more thoroughly than I shall ever now be able to do again particular parts of the city. What I have attempted is a synthesis, a portrait of a city growing, and extending, layer upon layer, for nearly two thousand years. I have attempted, by selection and generalization and by some imaginative interpretation of facts and records, to bring a mass of data together in one conspectus.

Certain aspects of that conspectus ought to be emphasized. I discovered early on, by mapping the main lines of the city in different periods on transparent overlays, that there was a vivid coincidence of its urban structure in all those different periods. Even where major interruptions had taken place the builders of York had constantly returned to the same lines and used again the essential geography of the city, sometimes leap-frogging a period and picking up pieces of an earlier one. Almost uncannily the city of York reveals its continuity. But it is not just a superficial or 'end-on' continuity, with periods following one another as if in a straight line; it is basic, central and fundamental. The same core dies and is reborn again and again.

The most dramatic example of that is the history of the secondary river in the city centre. The story of the river Foss could have been taken as the key to the development of the city. A look at the plans that accompany the text will reveal how much the river has been pushed around, modified and used and how much that has reflected the changing fortunes of the city as a whole. Its manipulation suggested, along with many other changes, the division of the book into broad periods. The story of York, I concluded, can be divided into seven main phases, each with distinct social and economic as well as physical peculiarities—not all of similar length or of equal effect upon the fabric of the city, but all capable of being defined and coherent in themselves. In each phase there has been a dominant building or urban area; I have therefore divided the book into seven chapters each identified by a major construction or place which is identified with the most characteristic activity of its time.

Finally, I make no claim for the scholarly fastidiousness of this study. The test I have used throughout for the validity of any conclusions is not documentation; it is my own detailed knowledge of the physical reality outside. I have attempted to ask myself, while looking and wandering about, feeling and hearing and smelling the place, whether what I have described was possible, whether it must in any case have happened and what it must have looked like when it did. In that sense I have been looking at the city as an architect, fascinated by appearances, constantly trying to provide dates and descriptions, attempting to understand the totality of a building or a scene and all the time concerned with the function of the building, or, in this case, of the town. An understanding of that function must surely create a keener enjoyment of what one is looking at. That certainly is what has happened to me. I hope that this book will open up a few windows for others as well.

PART OF THE KINGS MANOR

1. *The Legionary Fortress*

Some time in the summer of the year A.D. 71 part of a Roman legion, moving up the river Ouse, reached a widened stretch of water where it swung to the west and was joined by the river Foss; they decided to pause and set up camp on the tongue of land that separates the two rivers. Perhaps they had come by boat and the tide was going out; for the river was still tidal for another few miles. Perhaps their colleagues in the legion had been marching northwards along the bank and they met there. Perhaps they had come by land themselves, though that seems to me unlikely. Whatever the immediate reason and however they got there, they made a momentous decision, whose long-term effects are with us still.

It is all the more remarkable, because to the legionary standing on that tongue of land there cannot have been much of obvious significance in the scene that met his eyes. There were almost certainly no dwellings; there are no records or remains of any. What he saw instead was a fairly wide untidy river with ragged grassy banks partially eroded and showing alluvial silts where the tide had stripped them bare. Where he had landed there was a swamp, with rushes and reeds and tangled vegetation, and across the river, to the west and south, there were almost certainly more of them. To the north, some distance away, lay a forest with oak and birch and alders in the swampier patches: around him bushes and ferns and reedy pools, the noise of sandpipers, wild ducks, mallards, curlews and moorhens. At its best it cannot have been a hospitable scene. And if it was misty, damp and drizzling, as it probably was, he can hardly have felt a surge of optimism or had any hint of the place's future.

It was a land with configurations caused by moraines. But if it was bare near the banks there must have been trees nearby. The ground rising to a fairly level plateau on the left bank of the main river was probably crowned by yews, and it was the yews that had caught the eye of the legion's perceptive commander. Dark and evergreen, they may have indicated

19

a place used by the Britons as a place of worship and therefore accessible from many directions. Whatever their origin they were recorded in the name of the place where the commander decided to set up camp. For *Eboracum* was the Roman adaptation of the name given to the place by the Britons, *Eburacon*, which means either the place where the yew trees grow or a place belonging to someone called Eburos. And since someone called Eburos has not appeared in history either here or anywhere else and there is no evidence whatever for his existence, we may reasonably send him back into the obscurity from which he has so hesitantly emerged and assume the presence of the yews; as the camp was transformed, first made permanent and then a legionary fortress, it was called after them—*Eboracum*.

To found a fortress and ultimately a city at a junction of two rivers and the crossing of a major one was characteristic of the Romans as well as being typical of the founding of most of the major cities of the world. Most of them were originally set down at a river crossing, at the place of intersection of major roads or—even more significantly—at the place on a river which is the highest point to which ships can ascend. That place is most conveniently a little below the limit of the tide. At such a place it is possible to create a port away from the coast, in touch with the overland routes, safer than it could ever be on the coast. For the tide acts in two ways: it brings ships in and also keeps them out and makes for better defence. Of that situation York was a perfect example. It was tidal until a weir was built a few miles downstream at Naburn in the eighteenth century.

In the replanning and organization of the north of England initiated by the Roman forces of occupation, rivers played a constant and significant part. The navy, the Classis Britannica, operated up and down the east coast. It was presumably waiting in the estuary of the Humber and shipped the army across to march further north to Malton (Derventio). It may have moved up the river as well.

At the point where the camp was established, it commanded not only major routes by water to many parts of the country but also a whole network of communications over land. The establishment of the camp at York was thus an example of the Roman genius for strategical planning; as they built their straight roads across the contours and linked up the major centres the fortress became a centre for offensive campaigns against the tribes of the north and—possibly more important—a secure base for supplies, for the planning of operations and for the logistical exercises at which the Romans were unrivalled.

Looking at the map today it is possible to see more easily what the legion's commander appreciated at the time. The Ouse connected with the Humber and therefore with the North Sea, thus providing access by water to the south and east as well as to the north. By land there were communications everywhere—to Lincoln, from which the legion had set out, and to the other major towns—to Leicester, to Colchester, to Gloucester and to London. To the north-east there was access to the sea at Scarborough, where the Romans set up an early warning station on the edge of the cliffs; to the north there was access to the settlement at Aldborough (Isurium Brigantum) and thence via Catterick to the northern regions, to Hadrian's Wall (later) and to Scotland. To the south-west a direct route led to another major camp at Chester and connected to the roads on the western side of the Pennines. To the north the road reached Stanwick and crossed over Stainmore towards Brough, following a line across the moors with regular stations set a day's march apart.

So skilful was the organization of the communications, and so geometrical the layout of those straight roads, defining a system of land distribution which the Romans applied widely throughout their Empire, that it is tempting to see the planning of the roads of Britain as part of a huge geometrical exercise. It has even been suggested that since the Fosse Way runs north-eastwards in almost a straight line from the south-west to Lincoln and since it is met almost at right angles at Leicester by the road leading to Colchester, one of the four main civilian settlements, there might be evidence of formal regional planning on a huge scale. Similarly there is an almost straight line formed by the more northern roads running from south west to north east and connecting settlements in Wales, Chester (Deva), Manchester (Manucium), Tadcaster (Calcaria), York (Eboracum), Malton (Derventio) and finally Scarborough.

It may be that the line of the main routeways influenced the direction of the roads leading from them, as it seems to have done at York. But there are equally likely explanations. The south-west to north-east orientation of the roads reflects the basic geography of the island, influenced by the prehistoric movement of the glaciers; it is also the line of some of the main valleys and of ancient trading routes across the Pennines to Scandinavia. From the Cotswolds to Yorkshire it is the line of the oolitic limestone which has inspired some of the most distinctive buildings in these islands. But essentially the line of the roads and the location of the settlements indicates the evolving pattern of Roman occupation as the army worked its way northwards from the south-east.

The first raid made by the Romans on Britain was Julius Caesar's in 55 B.C. For nearly a hundred years after that they kept deliberately away, being occupied by other matters. It was not until A.D. 43 that four legions under Aulus Plautius landed at Richborough in Kent, defeated the Britons and moved rapidly to Colchester, with a view to a total occupation of the island. Although it was far from the heart of the Roman Empire, which in its most developed form encircled the Mediterranean seaboard, Britain was a constant irritant politically as well as being the source of important minerals that the Romans could usefully exploit. By the year 47 they had established fortresses at Lincoln and Gloucester and were in control of the island south of a line from the Humber to the Severn.

The largest of the tribes beyond that line, in the largest of the territories stretching from the Trent to the foothills of the Cheviots, were the Brigantes. The Romans made an alliance with their queen Cartimandua, who seems to have been one of the less attractive personalities of her time, and that kept affairs relatively stable for a few years. But in A.D.

69 she fell out with her husband Venutius, who took over the area of the Brigantes, drove Cartimandua out and built a colossal fort at Stanwick, nor far from Richmond, whose remains indicate something of its scale and the elaboration of its defensive system.

It was the settling of this rebellion and the defeat of Venutius that led to the founding of Eboracum or York. One of the commanders of the Roman army in Britain in the forties had been Vespasian, who had now returned to Rome. After a catastrophic year in A.D. 69 when there were four emperors in quick succession, Vespasian took over and established himself as Emperor. Having put down revolts in Judea and on the Rhine he turned his attention to Britain and to the need to bring it within the full jurisdiction of the Roman empire. To carry out this task he appointed as Governor a former colleague, Quintus Petillius Cerialis who had fought in the British wars at the time of Boudicca's rising in 61. Cerialis lost no time. He set sail in the spring of 71, taking with him the Second Legion Adiutrix from Holland and established them in Lincoln. From Lincoln he took the Ninth Legion Hispana and moved north.

He was an energetic, ruthless and efficient man. In the three years from 71 to 74 he defeated the Brigantes, captured Stanwick, and made York the principal military centre of northern Britain. His successor was able within a few years to set up two other permanent fortresses, at Caerleon in Monmouthshire and at Chester. But Cerialis had set the pattern; it was his decision that led to the establishment of the legionary fortress and then the civilian town, and it was that fortress which gave definition and form to the later development of the city.

The fortress was laid out on the plateau on the left bank of the Ouse, its orientation following that of the main roads going through it and past it. In plan it was of roughly playing card shape with rounded corners, fifty acres in area. It was enclosed and defined by defensive walls, at first built quickly on a foundation of timber boughs, with a clay rampart and a turf front. During the governorship of Agricola, between 79 and 85, the walls were completed, with a new foundation of squared oak beams, and a solid rampart of clay with turf facing lapped by a timber palisade. At intervals there were towers, of timber, wattle and daub and shingle roofs. Under the Emperor Trajan, between 107 and 108, the defences were rebuilt, this time in stone, so that York became more formidably the third of the major fortresses that included Caerleon and Chester. About the year 200 another major rebuilding occurred; and then another again about a hundred years later. This was a radical recasting of the defences. There were now stone walls about twenty-one feet high and five feet thick of white magnesian Tadcaster limestone, with tile through-bands and a tile cornice, and an earthern rampart inside.

What made it especially impressive was the line of towers along the walls at intervals, at first almost flush with the outside of the walls and projecting inwards, later projecting dramatically outwards. In the centre of each wall was a great gate—the Porta Principalis (where Bootham Bar is now) built of gritstone blocks with a central carriageway and pedestrian paths on each side, the Porta Principalis Sinistra (where King's Square is now, its name testifying to the fact that later the palace of a Danish king was constructed from it), the Porta Decumana (of which nothing remains) on the north-east side and the magnificent Porta Praetoria on the south-west side facing the river, flanked on each side by three interval towers and a huge multangular tower about 60 feet high at each corner, one of which survives in Museum Gardens, with mediaeval additions forming the top layers. That front had a splendour almost unique among Roman camps; there was nothing in the British Isles to rival it. It must have been intended to demonstrate that this was by now the headquarters of the Dux Britanniarum, the commander in chief of all the military forces in Britain.

The size and layout of the camp as a whole was determined by its being the base for a legion, the major unit of the Roman army. A legion was subdivided into centuries of 80 men, led by a centurion. Six centuries formed a cohort and ten cohorts formed a legion. The fortress therefore accommodated about 6,000 men, including the legionaries, over a hundred horsemen and the auxiliaries (archers, slingers and others, often forcibly recruited and gaining citizenship after twenty-five years' service). In addition to specialist officers such as surveyors, doctors and clerks, there were six tribunes to each legion, usually young men under twenty-five years of age, at the first stage of their careers as politicians.

The main gates controlled the main roads of the camp, with names corresponding to those of the gates. From the great Porta Praetoria, the Via Praetoria led past rows of timber-framed barrack blocks to the heart of the fortress. There it was crossed at right angles by the Via Principalis. Along that were the houses of the tribunes. At the junction of the two roads in the centre and facing down the Via Praetoria was the Principia, the headquarters of the legion, an imposing group, with a courtyard and colonnades, a basilica, offices and stores. It must have been at least as big as the present Minster nave.

That basic layout survives. For though the Porta Praetoria has entirely disappeared, enough of the walls remain, either beneath mediaeval walls on the north and west or more vividly in the form of the great Multangular Tower, to indicate the shape and character of the fortress. The Via Praetoria is Stonegate (at least six feet below the present level), the Via Principalis is Petergate; and at their crossing, the Minster stands over the Principia. In the new crypt formed by the recent restoration below the central tower you can now see some remains of the walls of the Roman headquarters.

It must have been a thriving and active military centre, crowded with soldiers and administrators busy with the constant work of that army—surveying, building roads and bridges, constructing water supplies and canals, continually developing new technologies. The praetorium, the commander's house, stood somewhere presumably near the centre. There were granaries, workshops, stables, cookhouses, a hospital and, of course, the inevitable baths, the remnants of one of them still below an inn in St Sampson's Square. And below it all, revealed in one of the most spectacular archaeological discoveries of recent years, was a solidly built and generous system of sewers to all parts of the fort.

But it would be an incomplete picture to imagine only the enclosed legionary fortress on one bank of the river. From the beginning there were other buildings and functions outside the walls. To the north-west and the south-east *canabae*, or booths, were built; and land was brought under cultivation, as farms and woodland, on short leases, constantly pushing out and following the roads in a ribbon development as it usually does still today.

The main harbour lay on the Foss, a short distance south-east of the fortress. At a bend in the river it was lined with quays and wharves and a tower crane stood on a stone base. To and from that harbour came the voluminous trade of the settlement, in contact with the Continent, especially the Low Countries and France, via the North Sea, and with the rest of Britain via the Aire and the Wharfe, the Ouse, the Trent and the Carr and Foss Dikes— a trade of wine and grain, of stone and pottery, of jewellery and cloth, of corn and coal and lead and gypsum.

To the south-west, facing directly the great Porta Praetoria, a wooden bridge spanned the Ouse and led to the main street of a separate settlement that acquired increasing importance with the years. That civil town, which was probably as big as the area now enclosed by the mediaeval walls, was at first the kind of settlement that inevitably grows up in the wake of an army—of tradesmen and suppliers and camp followers. But increasingly it was occupied by retired soldiers; on retirement after fourteen years in the ranks and four as veterans, legionaries received good pensions and usually grants of land and a bonus. By that time the members of the army of occupation had in many cases married and settled down. In any case, by the time the Roman occupation came to an end, legions in places like York were recruiting locally second and third generation soldiers, descendants of men who had settled there on retirement and who had grown up in the country as Roman citizens.

By the second century the civil town was growing rapidly. In 213 it was given the status of a *colonia*, making it one of the four main Roman civil towns—York, Gloucester, Colchester and Lincoln. That probably coincided with the promotion of the city as the capital of *Britannia Inferior*, the epithet indicating not its reputation but the fact that the Romans looked at Britain upside down from the way we do; inferior implied the part furthest from Rome itself. The governor had his residence in the civil town and the praetorium may have been there, unless it was in the camp. There was also a *domus palatina*; for several Roman Emperors spent some years in residence. The Emperor Septimus Severus lived in the town from 208 to 211 while he was directing campaigns in northern Britain. He died there. So in 306 did the Emperor Constantius Chlorus. His son Constantine was proclaimed Emperor; he was to become Constantine the Great and to change the official religion of Rome to Christianity.

The *colonia* must have presented a vivacious and vigorous urban scene, the very picture of what Professor Richmond has described as a bustling and confident world. With a population of probably more than 6,000, it was a very cosmopolitan place. There was a large temple to Serapis, there were huge public baths, a great colonnaded basilica (in what is now Hudson Street) combining the law courts and the town hall. The land was partly terraced as it rose up the hill from the river. The houses were mostly packed fairly tightly in blocks not much more than 120 feet wide. They lined the main roads, particularly the route that led directly south-westwards to Tadcaster and Manchester. Along what is now Toft Green were some of the better houses, grouped around courtyards, with mosaic floors and under-floor central heating. Bustling it certainly must have been, with booths and shops, bronze workers and jewellers (a speciality of York being the jet from Whitby), with houses of white stone with red tiled roofs, with piped water supplies and fountains and cisterns set up in the cobbled streets.

Along the main road and in the part of the city just outside the walls where the station is now were the cemeteries and their monuments. Further out were villas and farms and the bigger estates, a landscape of stone-surfaced roads with dirt tracks leading off them to the farmhouses, with hedges and windbreaks of oak and birch, and gardens with pansies and lilies and poppies. It was a landscape of farms, mostly arable, supplying the wheat which the government was continually demanding: but also pastoral, with large herds of cattle in the fields and pigs in the forests. It must have seemed as secure, as well organized and as permanent as at any period of the island's history.

Yet by the time all this was in being, it was already beginning to decline. It is clear from recent evidence that although the fortress itself and most of the civil town was above flood level the constant silting up of the river by the beginning of the fifth century caused a series of disastrous floods. By that time the political situation was already out of hand. The control and administration of the regions further north had begun to break down.

In the second century the Roman *imperium* had been methodically extended. Hadrian's Wall was built across the narrow neck of northern Britain between 122 and 128. Ten years later, much further north, the erection of the Antonine Wall was begun across the narrowest part of Scotland between the Forth and the Clyde. But in 155 that wall was abandoned and Scotland evacuated. In 197 Hadrian's Wall was destroyed. It was rebuilt and reoccupied ten years later by Septimus Severus. By then the Ninth Legion had been replaced in York by the Sixth and had been moved away to the eastern part of the Empire where it disappeared or was disbanded. Hadrian's Wall was destroyed again in 296 and 367. Finally in 410 the Emperor Honorius instructed the Britons to look to their own defence. An era had come to an end.

It has been worth spending some time on Roman York because of its ultimate significance. For it was the key position of York in a network of communications that caused its foundation and its subsequent history. That legionary fortress is still the centre of the city. The junction of its principal roads is still its heart—at Minster Gates. The roads connecting to them (at first through great portals in the centres of the walls) are still the main routes to and from York—from Scotland, from the Pennines, from the coast, from the Humber, from the Great North Road and the south. And as the fortunes of the city changed and shifted, as it waxed and waned in political and economic significance, that fundamental position as a centre of communications was retained. When the railways came they found (with a little disreputable help) a natural centre in York. And a centre is what it still is— once for a Roman army, now for a resident population and a new army of visitors.

Nineteen hundred years after the founding of the city by a Roman army, the drums of a Roman column were discovered among the foundations of York Minster. In 1971 the column was erected again near Minster Gates—a symbol of the continuity of development and design that makes York more readily legible as a historical document than any other settlement of its antiquity.

2. The Market

The departure of the Romans after 410 and the gradual unwinding of their system of administration marked the beginning of a period in York's history about which too little is known for certain but discoveries are quickly being made. It is the period generally known as the Dark Ages, a name which tends to divert attention from the fact that the darkest thing about the period is our ignorance of it rather than anything inherent in its character. In York that darkness was partly caused by a disastrous destruction of its records shortly after the Norman Conquest of 1066. For a period extending over six hundred years it is therefore not easy to speak with certainty or precision. Nor does any account of the political state of the region during that time make a clear picture any easier to draw.

Yet it was possibly the most definitive and influential span of time in the city's history, at least as far as the city itself is concerned. And that can be assumed even though there is an extraordinary lack of buildings of that period. The obsession of most historians until recently with political history often obscures the realities, affecting the daily life of every man, of the periods with which they deal. But those realities can be inferred, and evidence of them can be either dug up (in this case not very much) or deduced from a study of what records exist; still more significantly, they can be grasped from the evidence in the city itself, its shape and form. For what the period discussed in this chapter left to York was nothing less than an urban structure and form that continued and was established even more firmly in later centuries.

Before looking at that it is necessary to summarize briefly the main groups of events between the departure of the Romans and the dramatic arrival of the Normans six hundred and fifty years later.

The hundred years immediately following the Romans' official departure was a time of relative peace. Caer Ebrauc, the Romano-British settlement that was really a kind of relaxed Eboracum, must have remained essentially similar to it. But in 525 the fortress, still remaining and still used, was captured by Anglians during one of the invasions by Anglo-Saxons from Germany that dominate English history of the fifth and sixth centuries. They came up the Humber, destroyed the old wooden bridge and drove the British back to the small kingdom of Elmete, west of York, which survived for a century and was only incorporated into the Anglian kingdom in 626. The Anglian kingdom of Deira was centred in the wolds of the East Riding, so that York itself was effectively on its edge. It was a kingdom of many villages and few towns. York was one of them—Eoforwic, a name that it now adopted and was eventually transformed into the present one.

In 625, exactly a hundred years after the Anglians' arrival, the situation was transformed again. For in that year King Edwin, who had been born in 585 and taken over the kingdom in 617, married Ethelburga, the sister of the King of Kent, and brought her north to York. It was a turning point. Ethelburga was a Christian, her family having been converted to Christianity by Augustine, the missionary who, sent to England by Pope Gregory the Great, had landed in Kent in 597. With Ethelburga came Paulinus, her chaplain, and an agreement that the Queen would be free to practise the Christian religion. Within two years Edwin had decided to join it too. On Easter Day 627 he was baptized in a small wooden church hastily erected in the street adjoining his palace (the old Roman praetorium, or part of it) and dedicated to St Peter. That church, later enclosed in stone and completed after Edwin's death, was either on the site of the present Minster nave or somewhere to the west of it. Whatever its site, it was the origin of the Minster.

It was also more. It symbolized the establishment of York as a major unit of the western Church as well as the centre of a kingdom. For while Edwin made York the capital of his kingdom, Paulinus, as archbishop, made it an ecclesiastical capital. In 601 Pope Gregory had sent the pallium to St Augustine. In the letter that accompanied it he outlined the basic ecclesiastical system. He visualized two sees, York being the northern one, with twelve bishoprics. It was to be a metropolitan see; and although it did not in fact receive metropolitan status until 735, it moved steadily in that direction under Edwin and Paulinus. It has been said that that event was the most permanent legacy of Eboracum, the return of Roman civilization in peace.

If the transformation of York into the ecclesiastical capital of the northern region inaugurated one of the great periods of church development, that was in no way reflected by the political events of the next few centuries. In 633 Edwin was killed in the battle of Hatfield near Doncaster. After an unpleasant interlude of a year his throne was taken over by another outstanding king, Oswald. He ruled the kingdom from Bamburgh and was responsible for bringing Aidan to Lindisfarne in 634. It might therefore seem that York would become a bywater.

In fact it became something very different. Despite the confusion, turbulence and bewildering changes that made the political history of the next two hundred years a nightmare of transient names and changing fortunes as one leader after another murdered and fought his way to temporary power, the actual life of the city enjoyed one of the brightest periods it has had in its history. It was the period of its greatest learning and the growing authority and influence of the Church—an authority that can be seen, in very contrasted ways, in the lives and careers of two outstanding churchmen of the seventh and eighth centuries.

The first was St Wilfrid. Born in 634, Wilfrid studied under Aidan at Lindisfarne and went to Rome where he acquired a love and loyalty for Roman church organization that was to affect his life thereafter. He came to York in 658 and was made Abbot of Ripon in 661. At that moment the conflict between the practices of the Roman and Celtic churches came to a head. Wilfrid played a central part in the adoption of the Roman calendar and practice; the date of Easter was settled at the Synod of Whitby in 663. It was a more significant decision than it might at first appear. For it made possible the unification of Europe within the Roman rite.

Wilfrid was Bishop of York for two periods; from 669 to 677, and from 686 to 691. He seems to have been a tough, intolerant, opinionated and turbulent man. He was unusually quarrelsome, even for a clergyman, and seems to have been unable to avoid quarrelling bitterly with any king he dealt with. He was sent away twice and died in 709. But by that time he had repaired the Minster, which he had found with a leaking roof, without windows and with birds flying in and out; and he had glazed it for the first time. His quarrels kept him unusually fit. He survived to the age of 75.

The second was Egbert, one of the pupils of the Venerable Bede (673–735), who became primate of the northern province in 732 and archbishop of York in 735. It was under him that York began to take over from the more northern monasteries—at Hexham, Jarrow, Wearmouth and Lindisfarne—as the intellectual centre of the country, and in certain respects one of the intellectual and cultural centres of European civilization. A man of immense influence and effectiveness, Egbert reorganized the Minster after two disastrous fires and rebuilt it facing east and west. As part of that total reorganization he was responsible for founding the school and the library; and with that library, known as one of the greatest of its time and a source of inspiration for scholars, York replaced Jarrow as a centre of literary and educational enterprise.

Its luminary was Alcuin, born about the year Egbert took over the metropolitan see. In 767 Egbert's successor as archbishop put Alcuin in charge of the school and in 781 he became custodian of the library as well. His own work, encyclopaedic in scale and nature, gave him an international reputation as a scholar and administrator. In 782 he was invited to Charlemagne's court. He made a brief return to York in 786 and a longer one between 790 and 793. Despite his respect for it (he described York as *Emporium terrae commune marisque*—the common mart of sea and land) the general unrest deterred him from staying longer and he returned to the continent, to work in effect as Charlemagne's Minister of Education. He died at Tours about 804.

If York during the eighth century achieved a splendour symbolized by its new Minster and a prominence as a centre of learning that it was not to recover again until the twentieth century, it took on a very different character in the ninth century. In the midst of family and political troubles, it was a natural prey to anyone looking for aggrandizement and wealth. To the Danes, especially those landless younger sons who could not inherit property and made their fortunes by raiding at sea and creating new markets, York must have seemed an enviable prize.

The first raids by the Danes on England were made in 787. Then there was a pause. After 832 they raided mainly on the south-west coast, moving in the fifties and sixties to Sussex and Kent and thence to East Anglia. In 867 they sailed from East Anglia up the North Sea, along the Humber and the Ouse under their leader Ivar the Boneless and captured the city in a ferocious battle.

The Danes must have arrived at high tide; when the river in York was tidal, it must at low tide have been muddy at the sides and impassable. They came up the river in long-boats, undecked, with a square sail and lines of oarsmen along each side. They had 350 ships a few years previously and there is no reason to doubt that they used them again. Some of the Danes may have stopped at the end of the estuary at Barton and have come across land to take the city in a pincer movement as the ships arrived by river, all on one tide, a line of boats between two and four miles long. It must have been a bewildering and awesome sight as ship after ship moored and the oarsmen, seizing their shields from the sides, raced into the city.

It was the end of the Kingdom of Northumbria and the start of a Danish kingdom that had strong links with Scandinavia on the one hand and with Ireland on the other, the king of Dublin at the time being the Dane who had captured York. The city's name changed again, this time to Jorvik. But the Danes, like many victors in history, were as much taken over by the city as the city taken over by them. By the eighties it was a Christian city again. But it was more. It became the major trading centre of the country, with routes south-west through Chester to Dublin and across the sea to Denmark, Norway and the Low Countries.

It did not survive very long in that form. In 927 Athelstan, the king from the south, annexed York. There followed twenty-eight years of conflict, none of them more colourful than the short reign of the Viking Eric Bloodaxe, who appeared about 947, was expelled in 948, reappeared in 952 and ruled for two years before finally being expelled in 954 and murdered in a battle at Stainmore. With the expulsion of Eric, described as a 'bad-minded, gruff, unfriendly and silent' man, although a much admired warrior, the Danish kingdom came to an end eighty-seven years after the capture of York. England became at last one realm and for over a hundred years York was part, no longer of a local kingdom, but of the northern earldom which was part of that realm, its chief city and the residence of the earls. For a time under Canute, who took over the crown in 1016, England was part of a much greater unified kingdom which included Denmark and Norway; the northern earldom continued in that context.

The change from that system leads into the next chapter. The remainder of this one is concerned with the physical development of the city in the years discussed above.

If there are few monuments of the period there is very real evidence of the growth of the city. That happened possibly rather more during the Danish ascendancy than in the Anglian era. For the Anglians were not really an urban people. They set up the main part of their kingdom in the wolds of the East Riding and only gradually moved across to the Vale of York. Their settlements were generally not so much towns—and certainly not cities—as villages. In the area surrounding York, within a radius of about ten miles, there are at least seventy or eighty of these villages, with names often ending in -wic or -ton or -ham, founded during that era and named after activities or kinds of tree.

The city itself cannot have changed significantly in the aftermath of the Roman occupation. The fortress stood, its defences still in existence but noticeably decaying with the years. A few repairs and improvements were made, notably the Anglian tower in the north-west stretch of the fortress wall, a simple rectilinear tower of rough stone built sometime in the seventh century. The Minster was begun and so were some of the parish churches, built mainly of wattle or timber and thatch. The old barracks within the walls must have been used, and presumably the buildings surrounding and forming the praetorium were used also; the early minster with its library and school were erected there.

But the simple geometry of the fortress was undoubtedly modified. New tracks were made, following functional needs rather than the grain of the fortress with its main axes at right angles to each other. These diagonal pathways, roughly parallel to each other, may have established in an irregular way the lines that later became Goodramgate (joining the south east and north east gates): Feasegate and Grape Lane (joining the south east corner to the centre): Blake Street and the much later St Leonards Crescent (joining the main gate to the north-west gate). As the routes became established, the main axes of the city probably shifted in emphasis. The old Via Praetoria, on the line of Stonegate, following the main grain of the country and the Roman roads, probably became less important, as its way was increasingly impeded by the Minster and associated buildings.

The old Via Principalis, on the other hand, became more important. It led to the most significant extension of the city: that is, the space between the Ouse and the Foss southeast of the fortress. It was during this time that the chief market of the city moved to that area, near the landing places on the two rivers. In that great market all sorts of produce were bought and sold. There were also slaves. It may have been here that the slaves were bought by Romans whose fairness and beauty attracted Pope Gregory in Rome and inspired him to send a mission to England.

From that market a road crossed over the front of the old fortress, on a line that became Coney Street. And it must have been because of the market that a new and increasingly important route was gradually developed, following a natural line across the river to join the line of the old Roman road near the later Micklegate Bar. Was there a bridge where it crossed the Ouse? It has often been suggested that there was not, that there were merely stepping stones at low tide. That would indicate that at low tide York was singularly empty of water and that the Ouse did not provide much. It seems to me unlikely. There must have been a bridge, presumably of timber, which was later replaced. The line of the road was basic to everything that later happened to the urban structure; it became Micklegate, the great street.

Across the river may have been the Archbishop's Palace. The land belonged to him and the name Bishophill may indicate that his palace was built on that ridge within the old colonia of the Roman occupation. It seems a natural place to put it because beyond it was the defensive ridge now marked by a later wall. In the houses and villas left by the Romans lived the thegns, the richer merchants and the freemen.

But it was really in the Danish period that the city took on much of the shape and urban character that it has today. The Danes had arrived by river and the river became for them, as it had been for the Romans, of crucial importance. For the river brought, not just raiders for plunder, but trade. Traders meant towns, preferably fortified ones. The Danes were thus major figures in the development of an urban civilization. Their occupation and reorganization, however short, established the main lines of the city as such: its commercial life, its regional and national significance, and—most important of all in the context of this study—the organic, rambling, irregular, winding and unrectilinear character of the city that has survived and given shape to the city in all its later manifestations.

To get an idea of that city it seems easiest to imagine it as it must have been at the end of that period, either towards the end of the Danish kingdom as such in the tenth century or in that interlude under the Northumbrian earls before the Norman Conquest.

It was a substantial place, possibly a very big one. One account gives its population as 30,000 at the turn of the tenth and eleventh centuries. That was the estimate by the monk of Ramsey, writing a life of Bishop Oswald. It is usually discounted as a wildly exaggerated estimate. It certainly seems extraordinarily high in the light of the later population and the usual size of towns of the period; on the other hand York was a great metropolis and a huge trading centre. A more credible estimate is that the population at the time of the Conquest was nearly 10,000. If so, that still made it for its time a major settlement.

It is tempting to work out the significance of those numbers in relation to the geographical shape of the city. According to Domesday, there were in King Edward's time seven 'shires'. The exact location of the shires is uncertain; what is recorded is that the castle shire was 'wasted', that the archbishop's shire contained 189 inhabited *mansiones* and that the other five shires contained 1,418 *mansiones*. Professor Dickens estimates that there were therefore altogether about 1,800 *mansiones* in 1066, some containing more than one house, and that therefore the population may have been between 8 and 9,000. It could easily have been 10,000.

These figures can now be related to the land. The Roman fortress area was 50 acres, the Colonia about 60 acres, the Anglo-Danish extension — the great market area near the Foss and between the two rivers—has been estimated as occupying 37 acres. It is impossible to be precise about that, because there are no obvious boundaries and it may have extended to include much of the land around the later castle. My estimate is that the Danes could have used some 70 acres in that area. If so, the total area of Danish York was somewhere in the region of 200 acres. (Since mediaeval York, including the Walmgate area, enclosed in the thirteenth century, occupied 263 acres, that seems a reasonable guess; in fact, the following argument concerning the crowdedness and density of Danish York is reinforced if one takes the smaller area of 37 acres, making the city in all about 170 acres.)

Assuming that some areas, such as the cathedral precinct, were mainly occupied by church buildings with only a little residential accommodation—say over 20 acres—and that the market itself occupied up to 30 acres, we can deduct at least 50 acres from the total for public, commercial and industrial uses. Deduct a further 10 acres (less than 7 per cent) to allow for those little bits of land that are always left over however hard you try to use it all, and I estimate that there cannot have been more than 140 acres for residential and associated workshop development.

A population of 10,000 gives a net residential density of over 70 people per acre, which is nowadays called a medium-high density; a population of 30,000 gives over 200 people per acre, which is the density of Victorian slums or modern multi-storey housing. As a further check, assume that there were about five persons per house. Then a density of 70 means that there were 14 or 15 houses per acre, which is reasonable; a density of over 200 means that there were at least 40 houses per acre, which is not. Because if York was anything like other settlements of the type at the time, most if not all of the houses must have been single-storey. On the assumption that such houses were fairly long and narrow—say 40 by 18 feet—the higher population would have involved building houses over the whole of the ground, leaving only the narrowest of strips to squeeze between houses and into them.

So, it seems the higher population is impossible. But—and here the character of Danish York begins to emerge—even the lower estimate gives with a net residential density of over 70 people per acre, a very crowded site. For that density is acceptable with two- and three-storey housing. With one-storey houses throughout, it means that, allowing for roads between rows of houses, reasonable but not large strips between houses, with just enough space for a few sheds and piggeries and some patches of land for workshops, the whole city must have been densely developed, and must have been arranged in repetitive, tightly organized strips with a minimum of open space. All very monotonous to look at. Since, furthermore, the Danes did not build sewage systems like those of the Romans, and since there must have been lots of fires to warm houses as well as work the tanneries and ironworks, the visitor looking across the city on a damp November day in the tenth century must have been peering through smoke and fog, nauseated by the smell and almost incapable of finding his way.

The fact that there are hardly any architectural remains makes York in no way remarkable. The Danes did not leave architectural monuments of the orthodox kind; indeed they seem never to have developed an architectural style or even an architectural interest. In the case of York, the few accounts which survive confirm that it was not an impressive spectacle. The Icelandic sagas of the thirteenth century, based upon the poems of Egil, the Icelander who visited York about 948 and is said to have written his poem at great speed to avoid death, described the marshy character of the land around the city. 'York town,' he says, 'the dank demesne.' It sounds very probable; for to some extent a dank demesne is what it still is. In any case the land around it, to judge from the ample evidence of floods, must have been very marshy indeed.

On the other hand quite a lot of development must have taken place in the surrounding agricultural land. The old Roman road crossing from the south-west was still visible in the ninth century. Away from that road and at some distance from York were villages, mostly street villages with wide central roads for gathering together stock in the long central green. Near the villages were groups of farmsteads, where there are now often villages, separated by long stretches of forest and marsh. The region was still largely forested, the main forest being that of Galtres to the north of York. But the work of clearing forests had been accelerating. There is evidence of people draining land and dyking it, clearing timber and setting up a more organized field system, usually with four major open fields, with a moor or common, and leaving the meadows—the 'ings'—in the low lying land of the Vale of York.

In York itself the Danes left, not monuments, but an urban form. It can be read in the layout of the place, in the street and district patterns, and in the property divisions, many of the present ones being unchanged since Danish times. For in making York a centre of trade the Danes give to the city a new pattern of streets and their names. Such were Goodramgate, Feasegate and Micklegate. Micklegate indeed was part of the main Danish thoroughfare, running from the south-west, across the Ouse by Ouse Bridge, through High Ousegate and Pavement and then over the Foss at Layerthorpe before leading across country towards Malton. The markets were on that route or close to it, the main one probably being near All Saints Pavement, where the mediaeval market cross stood until the nineteenth century.

Of the trade and manufacture, plenty of objects survive. Excavations in the last hundred years have thrown up considerable numbers of items—combs in every stage of manufacture, beads, glass, amber and jet, bonework and other ornaments. There were tanneries and tan-pits in High Ousegate and then in Tanner Row near the river, making shoes, laces, belts, bags and gloves. Iron was smelted outside the south corner of the fortress, and knives, buckles, axes, hooks and nails were made. There was a substantial trade up and down the Ouse in skins and ropes and masts, in iron and steel, imported from Scandinavia, in spices from the East, in gloves and cloths, wool, wine and vinegar from the Low Countries, in manufactured cloths, jewellery, metal work and embroidery from York itself. And that trade put York, in one direction, in regular touch with Norway and Denmark, with Iceland and Scotland; and in the other direction, across the land towards the south-west, with Chester and Dublin and the Isle of Man. It was at this time that a burgher class, of traders and commercial men, began to live outside the city and use its markets. It was almost certainly at this period too that the Jews began to come to York, to promote trade and expand their activities in a way that was to lead to disaster in the twelfth century.

York, as the biographer of Bishop Oswald at the end of the tenth century recorded, was a seat of commerce, thronged with people and bustling with trade, even if the walls were in disrepair. At its heart were the landing places on the Ouse and the Foss and the markets. The principal landing place, which was established by at least the tenth century and continued into the nineteenth century, was the King's Staith on the left bank just below Ouse Bridge. There were others, one at the foot of Lendal, beside the present Lendal Bridge; the steep lane descending to the water beside the bridge was the original Lendal (the present Lendal being part of Coney Street). Further upstream there was another landing place at the foot of what was later called Marygate, leading to Earlsborough, the headquarters of the Earls.

From a study of these fixed points and the general shape of the town it is clear that the key to its form was the market. That market occupied the space between the original fortress and the confluence of the rivers. It therefore shifted the heart of the city towards the south east. It also made logical the transformation of the old gate from the fortress towards the market into a palace for the Danish king, and the subsequent positioning of the castle. Over forty street names in York end in 'gate', the old Norse word for a street, and the names indicate their function or their position, such as Ousegate and Nessgate. Their lines were functional, linking churches and houses, trades and rivers. As the level of the city generally rose, new streets were created linking the main functions. Feasegate and

Finkle Street indicate the routes from the markets to the old centre and the newer Minster buildings.

About fifteen feet below the present levels, there were stalls in what later became the Shambles, a fish market by the Foss, merchants' houses along the right bank of the Ouse in Skeldergate. And the river must have been spanned by a bridge. The most telling evidence of the general form of the city comes from the record that before the Norman Conquest York was divided administratively into seven 'shires', of which one was given over to the castles, another to the Minster and its associated buildings, and another to the market. 'Marketshire' had the main road going through it and that included Micklegate, linking the principal market with the main gateways and routes as well as to the landing stages, the river and the sea.

It seems likely that the position of the surviving city walls was simply confirmed. They may have been the same as in Roman times, the walls surrounding the colonia as well as the fortress. On the other hand they may have been made by the Danes. The construction of the mounds on which timber palisades and then stone walls were later built suggest that they could have been Danish. Again, they may have been Anglian. The mounds were fitted loosely around the city, enclosing the river and the markets. Their line was much as it is today except for a stretch of wall constructed in 1215 between Fishergate Postern and the Red Tower. It is clear that the remaining walls of the fortress on the west and north were still used. The south and east walls presumably disappeared at this time—a logical reflection of the changing centre of gravity of the city.

It is just possible—though unlikely—that the mounds of the two York castles, Clifford's tower and Baile Hill, preceded the Norman Conquest. If so, what William the Conqueror did after taking the city in 1068 and 1069 was simply to repair and complete the palisaded enclosure on top of the mounds. But the general consensus is that William built them, within the existing city walls.

The other major building of the end of the period similarly established the position of what was to be a key location in the Middle Ages. That was the residence for the Earls created in the tenth century outside the fortress walls on the north west roughly where the ruins of St Mary's Abbey and the Museum Gardens are now. On rising ground, it must have dominated the city. It filled the space between Bootham and Marygate and became known as Earlsborough. At its edge a church dedicated to St Olaf, now St Olave's, was founded about 1050 by Earl Siward, the most notable of the Earls.

That church was rebuilt several times later. But its origin is indicative of the fact that many of the churches of York were in existence before the Norman Conquest. The Minster had been rebuilt in splendid style at the end of the eighth century; Holy Trinity Priory was founded in the tenth century; and there were at least eight others.

So, what kind of city was it? Damp and dirty, dominated by the remains of a fortress and by the new structures of the cathedral and the palaces, it was still in terms of space and form a market or a series of markets, linked by winding tracks to each other and to the landing stages. The key to the markets was the main route from the south west to the north east, not following the original Roman axis but twisting away towards the river Foss and the main market area before heading out to Malton and the coast. Not only the markets but also most of the pre-Conquest churches were related to that route (St Olave's, away to the north west, was part of Earlsborough). The focus of the market was probably a space near the junction of Pavement, Ousegate and Coppergate, near All Saints Pavement, where indeed it remained for many centuries. In that area the main route was crossed by the road from the north to the Humber—the Roman Via Principalis—now also bending away to the market and passing close to the palace of the Danish king.

The roads, or tracks, established their own lines, following what are nowadays described as 'desire lines' through the built-up area. Mud and stones and occasionally paved with larger flags, they were thickest near the market and the landings, more spaced out around the Minster, in the area of the old headquarters of the camp now used by the Church. The life of the Church and of scholarship was just a little removed from the world of trade and commerce, always orientated towards the two rivers—not the rivers as we know them today, but, at low tide, high banks of shiny black mud.

Constantly growing and changing, it was a town of wood and wattle houses, densely packed and mostly single storey. Most tightly grouped near the market area, more freely near the Cathedral, and possibly moderately spaced in the old Colonia on Bishophill, they generally had their gables to the street, were long and narrow and timber framed, built of oak, with oak and birch branches and cloth and canvas and mud. Those houses, together with the sheds and shelters of the markets, must have given a predominant character to the Danish city. For the churches must have been similarly constructed and only occasionally of stone, without towers or spires and generally low. The palaces also cannot have been tall buildings, but sprawling enclosures. Only the Minster can have provided a major dominant, and even that a relatively humble one compared with the buildings that took its place after the Conquest.

In short, both in the tenth and early eleventh centuries, York was a spreadeagled, scrappy, smelly, noisy and noisome northern capital. It was full of people and animals, craftsmen and traders, a scene of business and bustle and money making and vigour. It was a kind of urbanism that in this country was displaced by a more solid kind in the next few centuries. It was the kind that you see in a fairground—with plots laid out in an apparently untidy manner which is actually very rational, based on ease of access and convenient circulation. It was a kind of bazaar, not rigorously planned but very workable. I suspect that to get an idea of it today one should go to the Middle East or to the East; I have explored markets in the Far East that were, I felt, more like pre-Conquest York than anything we have today. For it was overlaid, within a century, by a new and powerful tradition.

★   ★   ★

The end of the period, as far as York was concerned, was as tragic and bloody as it was definitive. In the space of five years much of the market city was swept away; only the basic form, more lasting than buildings and artefacts, was preserved.

Edward the Confessor died in 1066, leaving no direct successor but an undertaking that William Duke of Normandy should succeed him. Two contenders were the sons of Godwin, the Earl of Wessex, who had been Edward's chief counsellor. Tostig had ruled the earldom of Northumbria for ten years, but there had been a rising against him. His brother Harold, who assumed Edward's crown on the day after his funeral, agreed to his banishment. In September, Tostig, having made an alliance with Harold Hardrada, the king of Norway, sailed up the Ouse with over 300 ships, left the fleet at Riccall about eight miles south of York, and in a major battle at Fulford, just outside the city, defeated Earls Edwin and Morkere. Then, leaving the fleet at Riccall, they went to Stamford Bridge, within easy reach of York, to receive hostages. What they received instead was the army of Harold Godwinson, who marched rapidly through Tadcaster and York and met them at Stamford Bridge on 25 September. In that battle both the King of Norway and Tostig were killed, with about nine-tenths of their army; so few survivors were left that they were only able to man twenty-four ships to return across the sea.

Harold's victory was short lived. He was relaxing in York when he received news that William Duke of Normandy had landed at Pevensey on 28 September. He marched hurriedly south, met William at Hastings on Friday 14 October, was defeated and killed after a reign that had lasted exactly nine months and nine days.

For York the story ends a few years later. It was not until 1068 that William, having been busy in the west, reached the north to deal with a rising. On his approach, the citizens of York gave him the keys to the city and hostages. He quickly threw up a new castle between the angle of the Foss and Ouse, in doing so destroying all the houses in that district. He then moved out, leaving 500 knights as a garrison. In 1069 another rebellion took place; William returned, put it down and built a second castle on the other bank of the Ouse at Baile Hill. In September of that year a fleet of Danish ships sailed up the Humber estuary; the men disembarked, joined forces with their English allies and marched on York. In order to destroy houses that might shelter the enemy, the Norman garrison set fire to them. The flames spread and destroyed a great deal of the city, including the Minster, the famous library and all the city's records. Amidst the conflagration the city fell, the Normans were defeated, booty was taken to the ships and many people were killed.

It was the last straw. William, hearing the news, swore a terrible oath 'by the splendour of God' and moved north again. He bribed the Danes to go away and after three weeks at Castleford advanced to York meeting no opposition. He repaired the two castles, pacified the city and then, from York as a base, remorselessly and relentlessly carried out in the winter of 1069–70 what came to be known as 'the harrying of the north'. From the Ouse to the Tyne he marched and counter-marched and devastated the whole region, destroying houses and barns, crops and farm implements. In the famine that followed it has been estimated that 100,000 people died; and for years afterwards, as records such as Domesday Book reveal, the land between York and Durham was waste. William was said in his later years to have had twinges of conscience about it; whether he did or did not, it was a lastingly effective settlement of the political state of the north for many centuries. Out of the ashes of that destruction arose a new culture and a new city. But in those ashes lay the remnants of the library, the dust of one of the great centres of learning in the West.

3. *Motte and Minster*

The city that rose from the fire after 1070 was a new city on ancient foundations. Its fundamental form was already there: its key sites already fixed. What was involved was a reorganization of those sites. The fabric of the city was given a new unity and adjusted itself to fit within it.

However long it took to re-establish a thriving community, the physical changes began to happen very quickly. One year after the disastrous fire, in the interests of defence, control and coherent administration, the castle was either created on a new mound or given new defences, a demonstration of arrogance and isolation in the midst of a disrupted community. In 1070 the river Foss, straggling southwards past the east side of the castle to join the Ouse a little way to the south, and already spreading out east of the old Roman fortress in a marsh, was dammed so as to make a moat around the mound and its bailey.

The effect was to kill several birds with one stone. About 120 acres of land were flooded; many houses and two mills were destroyed and a major feature of the mediaeval town was created—the Kings Fishpool, supplying for several hundred years one of the most important elements in the mediaeval diet—fish. At the same time the castle took on the standard appearance and style of a basic Norman castle. The motte, the earthen mound, rose up from the water, encircled at the top with a wooden palisade and punctuated with wooden buildings. At its foot, spreading towards the south east but separated from the motte by a strip of water, was the bailey, the parade-ground and military encampment, a flat area ringed with buildings, surrounded also by a palisade and the moat. The road from the city, the line that was appropriately to become Castlegate, reached down from the centre and entered the bailey through a gate across a bridge over the narrower part of the moat. From the bailey another bridge led across the moat again, steeply up the mound to the defences at its top.

40

The motte can be taken as the starting point for the Norman and mediaeval city because it was effectively the first major dominant of that city. It symbolized the new urban organization of the capital of the north, looking out across it, bristling with menace and the ultimate power of the new king. At a time when much of York was devastated and when in any case the majority of the buildings were low, of one or two storeys, and temporary, of timber and mud and thatch, with only a few stone buildings among them, it must have been a continual presence and an ominous reminder. Which, after all, it was intended to be.

The philosophy it represented was not entirely new. Under Edward the Confessor, Norman ideas of administration and law had been introduced into England. He had given land to Normans, some of whom had built for themselves castles of Norman type. Many aspects of the feudal system had already been adopted by the time of the Norman Conquest. Edward had spent twenty-five years of his life at the court of the Duke of Normandy before ascending the English throne in 1042. What the conquest meant was that a process already started was brought suddenly to completion.

William the Conqueror's use of York was in every way typical of his radical restructuring of the political and military scene. He planted castles wherever he went, making them the core of his administration. Before the Conquest there were few castles in England and those were mainly Norman-type creations by Edward the Confessor. William made the motte and bailey castle, quick to erect and relatively easy to maintain, a standard feature—in some cases, like York, Norwich and Exeter, throwing them up within existing town walls, in others starting anew. By the time of his death England was controlled, or at least partly controlled, by hundreds of these castles.

The taking over and reorganization of York is testimony to the extraordinary efficiency and powers of decision of William—or of his first High Sheriff, William Malet. To have grasped the essence of the problem and sorted it out so quickly was the mark of a ruler who knew where he was going and was not going to be sidetracked. Perhaps that is why in York, which is not known for the quickness of its decisions or its rigour in applying them, William the Conqueror for long retained an evil reputation. In the early eighteenth century the author of *Eboracum*, Francis Drake, wrote of him with singular ferocity: 'nor was there ever a tyrant in the christian or pagan world, that exercised his power so much to the destruction of his fellow creatures, before or since.' His comments were provoked by William's destruction of the city, which Drake considered 'as fair as the city of Rome' before being burnt by the Conqueror.

The place that was to be rebuilt must have been desolate and depressing for many years. The long grass mounds of the walls sloped sadly around the town except on the south-east side, where a huge tract of land was now flooded and impassable. The great buildings had gone or were lying in ruins—the residence of the Earls, the palace of the

Danish king, the burnt-out Minster; of the one and a half thousand houses, over a half must have been deserted and derelict as well. Only in one place, on the Staith beside the river, was there anything like the life and activity of the former provincial capital. The river itself probably showed more signs of life than the streets; it was still busy with sailing ships and galleys, drawn up just below the old wooden bridge on the site of Ouse Bridge.

Over the whole city loomed the brooding presence of the castle, the headquarters throughout the twelfth century of the King's representative, the High Sheriff. Its present form is deceptive. For what the observer usually sees is only that part of it known as Clifford's Tower, a name given to the shell keep on top of the motte at a much later date. The Norman castle was much more extensive and essentially in two parts—the motte and the bailey, that is, Clifford's Tower (the motte) on the one hand, and the area surrounded by the Assize Courts, the Debtors Prison and the Women's Prison, the latter two now the Castle Museum (the bailey) on the other. The bailey is still partly surrounded by its own stone walls, in the same magnesian limestone as Clifford's Tower and the City Walls. Rather like those walls, because it has in more recent times been decapitated and cut off clean along the top, it seems relatively innocuous and ineffectual. It is a false impression. Francis Place's drawing made just before 1700 gives a more accurate impression of the whole of this great complex, in its time as overpowering and obtrusive as the famous castles of North Wales that have survived more completely. The fishpond, forming a great lake, spreads across the front of the fortress; grassy banks spattered with untidy trees and shrubs climb up to massive walls. The south gatehouse looms upwards, its archway pointed and squeezed between two great drum towers. At the far side, not visible in Place's drawing, the line of the road down Castlegate led across a stone bridge to another pointed archway between semi-circular towers, and, at the south angle, dominating Place's drawing, a round tower. The whole thing must have looked terrifying and grotesque in relation to the scale and character of the city as a whole.

The shell keep at the top of the mound, Clifford's Tower, was built in stone between 1245 and 1262. Known throughout the Middle Ages as the 'great tower' it seems to have spent most of its life in a state of disrepair, not helped by the habit of some later occupants of taking bits down and selling the stone. In its crazy and apparently perilous way (a great crack on the east side which makes the south end lean outwards between two and three feet is less alarming than it seems; it has been there since the fourteenth century), the tower is still carelessly impressive. Its plan is quadrilobate, with four interpenetrating lobes; now a roofless shell, it was originally a two storey tower with a forebuilding restored in the seventeenth century. That forebuilding contained a chapel on the first floor and a small room above it housing the windlass for the portcullis. The main building contained four rooms on each floor around a central octagonal pillar which may have held up the fireplaces in the first-floor rooms. One of the lobes on the ground floor contained a well at least 46 feet deep. The tower was covered with a flat roof of lead, with a platform in the centre from which rose the chimneys and a flagstaff. And the whole building was strongly articulated; there are arrow slits, gunports and garderobe chutes in the outer walls.

It was gutted by fire in 1684 when a salute of seven guns had a greater effect than intended. That did not deter the military; another salute a few years later blew the gunner into the moat. But the tower was never used as a residence again and the whole castle gradually changed its role. The main alterations to the character of the place came in two stages: first, when the dam to the south east of the castle was altered in 1794 to allow the making of the Foss Navigation and finally in 1856 when the dam was removed altogether and the moat and fishponds were drained. But in its time the castle had served many purposes. It had been a fortress until the sixteenth century, a royal palace during the fifteenth, a mint, a prison, a court of justice, and—most important of all—the administrative centre for the county. The raven that lived in the tower and filled its spaces with its cries in the eighteenth century was a fitting manifestation for its declining years.

For the castle was the scene of the most disgraceful episode in the history of the city. By the twelfth century the Jews in York had achieved considerable significance in the commercial life of the city; and York, in company with many other places, experienced a wave of anti-Jewish agitation in the late twelfth century. In March 1190 riots flared. The Jews fled for sanctuary to the castle, those who did not reach it being either forcibly baptized or killed. For some reason which is not clear, but which led afterwards to his dismissal and punishment, the Sheriff ordered an attack on the castle. Some of the Jews in their terror committed mass suicide; those trying to escape were butchered. In the flames which consumed the tower and in the massacres outside about 150 Jews died.

The castle was more than a great defensive building; it was the hinge point of a total defensive system that enclosed the whole city. There were, to start with, two castles, one on each side of the river. They controlled movement at the city's most significant point—the junction of the Ouse and the Foss (Clifford's Tower) and immediately across the Ouse (Baile Hill) where the Old Baile was functioning by 1068 or 1069.

From the castles defensive mounds spread out to encircle the whole of the city. Parts of them at least were there before the Conquest. Immediately after it, following the example of the castles, they were capped with timber palisades. The long grassy mounds, with their timber tops, survived until the thirteenth century, when the city's defences were rebuilt and handsomely improved. Between 1250 and 1270 the timber palisades on the long mounds were replaced by stone walls with battlements and an encircling parapet walk. Those, however much restored, are essentially the walls that are still there, the most complete in the country on any scale. Only the walls of King Edward I's towns of Conway and Caernarvon are as complete; but the towns are much smaller.

The walls were built of the same magnesian limestone as the Minster, except for some gritstone on the bars. Only in one section was the wall incomplete. The King's Fishpool—nearly half a mile long and 400 feet wide—was quite impassable, a wide expanse of water, with fish and otters and ducks using it. The walls encircling the city stopped at its edge—on one side at Layerthorpe Postern, on the other at the Red Tower, a surprising little brick building with a pitched roof.

Next to that pool, the last part of the city wall to be built, surrounding the Walmgate area, remained capped with timber palisades until the middle of the fourteenth century. Including that part, the city walls enclosed 263 acres—a dramatic enlargement of the Roman fortress of 50 acres with its colonia of a similar size. Outside, on the north-west edge, the grounds of St Mary's Abbey, previously those of Earlsborough, were surrounded by walls in 1266.

The system was elaborate and impressive, the water of the moat around the castle and of the Fishpool controlled by the dam of Castle Mills, the mounds continuous and themselves descending to a ditch about 50 feet wide and 10 feet deep full of water, round the whole city. They had been made in 1216. (The work involved the removal of some houses outside the walls. The owners claimed compensation. Arguments were still raging nearly thirty years later.)

The city must have seemed impregnable. Where the walls stopped at the river Ouse, chains were slung across from tower to tower. On the main roads were the four bars; at the ends of the other routes and of the sections of wall were posterns—at North Street, Skeldergate and Fishergate, for example. And some roads changed their alignment because of the defences. Fossgate, once a straight line, the continuation of the Via Principalis of the Roman legionary fortress, now curved down to the south to cross the Foss at its narrowest remaining part and then curve back to its old line at Walmgate Bar.

Most of the walls are still there. Only in one place, St Leonard's Place, where the wall was breached to allow a new terrace of houses to be built in the nineteenth century, was the wall demolished. The impression the walls give today is the result of many centuries of change—of improvement as well as dereliction; but they remain one of the most complete and authentic urban monuments in the country, snaking walls of limestone, glittering in the sun, over two miles long on steep grassed banks punctuated by later planting, by limes and birches and beeches.

At their most complete they must have been spectacular. The great gates or bars—Bootham Bar, Monk Bar, Micklegate Bar and Walmgate Bar—were darker than the walls that met them, with taller battlements topped with strange threatening stone figures added in the seventeenth century; they contained dark chambers with arrow slits and winding gear inside, had portcullises and for many centuries each had a long barbican, a walled enclosure stretching out in front of the gateway like a roofless tunnel through which an attacker must hurry to reach the gate. Only one barbican survives (after protracted quarrels in the early nineteenth century)—the barbican at Walmgate Bar. The total losses to the walls since 1800 include 3 barbicans, 3 posterns, 5 intermediate towers and about 300 yards of wall.

The walls today fail to give an adequate impression of their original grandeur because of one important modification. Cut off at the same height as the rest of the wall, the intermediate towers are hardly visible except as protrusions and bays along the parapet walk. Those protrusions were not only significant features of the defensive system; above the level of the walls for most of their history rose 44 intermediate towers. They must have given an impression of power and security that the present walls, looking strangely small and decorative, cannot convey. To the traveller approaching the city they must have spelled watchfulness and an almost barbaric strength. Sadly it must be recorded that in the event the walls were not very effective. They were only put seriously to the test once, in the great siege of York in 1644 during the Civil War, and did not hold out for long.

The defences were the most obvious aspect of the city. And it is logical to look at them first; for one of the principal themes of the history of any mediaeval city—and York was no exception—was the change during the period from military rule to the dominance of commercial interests and the establishment of self-government. The following paragraphs trace that development, by looking in turn at aspects of the geography, politics, government, commerce, industry and population of the city.

The story of mediaeval York is its resurgence as the capital of the north and increasingly, especially during the wars with the Scots, its recognition as a key position in the strategy of the north of England. It had a crucial location on the rivers, which were navigable—both the Ouse and its tributary the Foss, at least as far as Layerthorpe Bridge—and on the roads. The main north-south route ran through the Vale of York, and from it still ran the routes to the east and to the south-west. As well therefore as a key military centre, York was the inevitable place for the market, not only for food and clothing but for heavier goods and raw materials; stone for example, was brought in from Cawood and Tadcaster, lead from Boroughbridge. From the eleventh to the fifteenth centuries York steadily increased in importance to become once again the greatest market of the north. William of Malmesbury, writing early in the twelfth century, was probably premature, but in relation to other places of the time tolerably accurate, when he described York as *urbs amplissima et metropolis*. It was, of course, a provincial metropolis. It is therefore necessary to look at it briefly in its regional context.

York was surrounded by villages, engaged in the farming of the land on the Anglo-Saxon open-field system, which survived through the whole of the Middle Ages. But the increasing source of wealth of the region—and vital to the wool trade in the city itself—was the series of huge sheep farms in the hills, mainly based upon the Cistercian abbeys. Yorkshire engaged in sheep farming on a scale bigger than anywhere else in England. At their peak the Abbey of Fountains had over 15,000 sheep, Rievaulx over 12,000.

Those abbeys were merely the largest and most prosperous of many. With Kirkstall in Leeds, and Jervaulx in Wensleydale, they represented the successful exploitation of the land by Cistercian monks in the twelfth century. There were innumerable other houses, of Cistercians and other orders—Benedictines, Premonstratensians, Augustinian canons and Carmelites, as well as the urban houses of the friars. Within a 25-mile radius of York, study of the map reveals at least 77 religious houses, not including smaller cells, granges, hermitages and chantries. They housed monks, canons regular, nuns, canonesses, friars, templars and hospitallers.

They seem to have grouped themselves by type. The Cistercians, Carthusians and Premonstratensians had a remarkable group about 30 miles north-west of York; the Augustinian canons, other orders and the nuns were more evenly spread around, mainly in the Vale of York, in the wolds and in North Yorkshire; the friars were in York itself.

If the religious houses dominated the geography of the region in one way, the castles dominated it in another. Again, Yorkshire fostered some of the biggest—Conisborough, Pontefract, Skipton, Spofforth, Harewood, Barden Tower, Ripley, Middleham, Helmsley, Pickering, Scarborough, Bolton, Lumley, Sheriff Hutton and many others. And from the fourteenth century onwards there were the fortified manor houses, like Low Burton Hall at Masham and Markenfield near Ripon.

The major buildings—castles, abbeys or manors—were nodal points in a developing rural scene that related to the major markets and the urban centres by generally inadequate communications. York was again essentially as it had been before, a key point in the system of roads as well as waterways.

The Norman administration inherited a collection of roads based upon the Roman roads, added to and elaborated by a tangle of tracks and field paths. The Normans laid down a standard width for a road under the king's protection; the main ones were based upon the great Roman roads—Fosse Way, Icknield Way, Ermine Street and Watling Street. They provided the major links between towns, but were not based upon London. Nor did the Normans move in that direction, perhaps partly because of the mobility of the early mediaeval monarchy. It was the growth of European trade as well as the growth of centralized government that gradually changed the pattern so that by the end of the Middle Ages the whole of England was within a fortnight's ride of London.

That affected York. For the main purpose of the major mediaeval roads was to unite markets with ports, and agricultural regions with markets. The local and regional roads emerged from demand and from use rather than from deliberate road making; they found their routes on prehistoric ridgeways, old Roman roads, along track and cartways and along the edges of fields. They were fairly flexible and changed their lines; more fixed and permanent were the bridges.

In such a situation York was of ultimate importance. The main road from London to the North ran several miles to the west, across Wetherby Bridge, keeping sensibly to the slightly higher and less easily flooded land. From that the old Roman road led to York itself, keeping to the prehistoric ridge on the moraine. Around the city, as the Gough map of about 1350 shows, there was a concentration of local and regional roads. There were roads leading from Leeming through Helperby to York, from York to Malton, from York through Pocklington to Market Weighton, from York to Howden, to Beverley and thence to Scarborough, Whitby and Guisborough: all of these in addition to the main routes such as the Great North Road and the radial routes from York to the north, east, south and west.

In addition there were the drove roads. The most famous was that across the Hambleton Hills, which according to tradition was followed by William the Conqueror on his way back to York from the north. It was certainly used by the Scots during the fighting under Edward II and Robert the Bruce. It passed by no less than five substantial monastic houses —Byland, Rievaulx, Newburgh, Mount Grace and the Convent of Arden at Hornby.

It was largely because of the roads that, after the reign of King John, who for some reason visited York almost annually and more often than any of his predecessors, the city came into prominence during the thirteenth century, with the intensification of the Scottish Wars. During them, for seven years, it effectively became the second capital of England. In 1298 Edward I transferred the Treasury to York from Westminster, along with the courts. It was convenient for his campaigns against the Scots; just as earlier York had been a convenient place for negotiations with the Scots, for royal weddings between the two countries and on one occasion for submission by the Scottish king.

That quickly changed. After 1304, when the Treasury was moved back to Westminster, York played a smaller part. The ill-fated Edward II paid it many visits and stayed there on his way to defeat at Bannockburn; but with the start of the Hundred Years War it was no longer in a key position.

York in fact only re-entered politics with the Wars of the Roses. For the man in the street the most visible evidence of those wars must have been the succession of heads decorating the main gates as fortunes changed and families made disastrous mistakes. After the Lancastrian revolt and the victory of Henry IV, several noble heads were set up on them, joined in the next few months by other heads sent back by Henry as he pursued his campaign through Northumberland. Then Edward IV defeated the Lancastrians (one of the crucial battles being at Towton in 1461, one of the bloodiest in English history) and Lancastrian heads replaced the Yorkist ones.

Among the heads put up on Micklegate Bar over the years were those of Sir Henry Percy (Hotspur) in 1403, Sir William Plumpton in 1405, Lord Scrope in 1415, the Duke of

York in 1460, the Earl of Devon in 1461 and the Earl of Northumberland in 1572. The last heads to be put on it were those of William Connolly and James Mayne in 1746; the last was taken down in 1754.

The end of the Wars of the Roses was one of York's sadder moments. Richard III seems to have won the affections of the citizens; he had been a regular visitor to York from 1475 and he and his wife became members of the Corpus Christi Guild in 1477. When Henry Tudor invaded England, the city sent eighty men to support Richard at the battle of Bosworth. They did not arrive in time. The mayor, who was at the battle, reported back on 23 August 1485 that 'King Richard, late lawfully reigning over us, was through great treason piteously slain and murdered, to the great heaviness of this city'. Nevertheless, the city, with characteristic care and caution, promised allegiance to the new king.

More significant was the city's own internal development in terms of self-government and trade. In the later eleventh and twelfth centuries York was ruled by the King through the High Sheriff. It received its first royal charter in 1154, but it was under King John that it began to achieve self-government. From 1212 it had its own mayor, then its own courts; by 1256 the city had acquired its own franchise and was answerable directly to central government. The thirteenth century thus saw its self-realization as a provincial capital. The change in emphasis was symbolized by the emphasis of new buildings. By the end of the Middle Ages authority was no longer hidden in the castle, which was actually visibly decaying, even though the Sheriff's offices were still there. It resided in two new buildings in the city centre—the Mayor's Chamber and the Council Chamber on Ouse Bridge and the Guildhall or 'common hall' of 1446–59 on the edge of the river on top of the old Roman approach road.

The mayor was the central figure and was proud of it; the man retiring from that post in 1501 recorded his achievements—new stocks, the repair of the walls, new weights for the common crane on Skeldergate, a new mace, two new fairs and the cleaning of the sewers. He might well be proud. For York at its peak was second only to London in its tax assessment. It maintained its level of prosperity through the fourteenth century when other places declined.

In the fifteenth century that situation reversed itself and by the sixteenth York found itself behind Bristol, Norwich and Newcastle, as well as possibly Exeter and Salisbury. The Golden Age of York was really between the middle of the fourteenth and the middle of the fifteenth centuries, and the basis of that was its prosperity. There was a highly profitable fish market on Foss Bridge as well as one at the foot of Ouse Bridge, a food market on Pavement, herbs at High Ousegate, wool on Ouse Bridge and in Walmgate, cattle both there and at Toft Green, pigs on Swinegate. Busier than all and geographically at the very centre of the enlarged city was the regular Thursday Market in St Sampson's Square. From York and the surrounding countryside people went there for meat, game and

1. Mediaeval York, with Motte and Minster

4. All Saints, North Street: the type of a mediaeval church

facing page
2. Petergate: the Via Principalis of Roman York
3. Stonegate: the Via Praetoria of Roman York

5. The Minster in its immediate setting

6. The Ascension: roof boss in the
   Minster nave

7. The West Front of the Minster

8. Roman York, with wall and Multangular Tower

9. The Minster: Choir after restoration

facing page
10. The Minster: looking up the Central Tower
11. All Saints, Pavement: the 15th century lantern
12. The Defences: 13th century city wall enclosing the Minster
13. The Castle: Clifford's Tower on its motte

10
11 12
13

14
15 | 17
16

14. The oldest houses in York: Lady Row, Goodramgate
15. Walmgate Bar: 14th century gate and barbican
16. The Merchant Adventurers' Hall
17. Lady Peckitt's Yard

18
19 | 21
20

18. The King's Manor: home of the Council
    in the North
19. The King's Manor: University of York
20. The Treasurer's House
21. Coffee Yard, between Stonegate and
    Swinegate

22. Shambles: the butchers' street

23. Shambles: from butchers to books

24. Tower Place: Regency elegance

25. The Debtors' Prison, once the finest gaol in Europe, now part of the Castle Museum

26. Ouse Bridge Inn, on King's Staith

27. The Assembly Rooms, social centre of Georgian York

28. Cumberland House, on the riverside

29. The Judges' Lodging, Lendal

30. Bishopthorpe Palace, the home of the archbishops of York
31. The Mansion House

32. The Railway Station

33. The Yorkshire Museum

34. Lendal Bridge

35. St Leonard's Place: Regency houses now Council offices

36. Prospect Place: 19th century workers' houses

37
38 | 40
39

37. Scarcroft School
38. University of York: the lake and college
39. University of York: staff houses at
   Bleachfield
40. New Earswick: the garden village

poultry, for salt herrings, butter and cheese and eggs, for salt and spices, for brushes and cups and dishes and bowls.

In the streets nearby, such as Shambles, but by no means restricted only to streets with a single trade, were shops occupied by a huge variety of craftsmen—leather and metal workers, pewterers, spurriers, lorimers, cutlers, bladesmiths, and, making a frightful smell, tanners. There were glovers, saddlers, skinners, hosiers, butchers, bakers, vintners and drapers: and the usual crowd of barbers.

From the list of commodities sold in York it is possible to draw a fairly clear picture of the commercial life of the city. It was at first a place for mainly consumption goods, for buying fish, grain and corn (from the city's mills), wine, meat, bread and salt. Increasingly it was a place to buy imported articles—cloth, swords, furs, wine and leather goods.

As the crafts developed, more of the articles on sale came from the locality or were serviced there—brass, wax, resins, oils, glass and pewter, boots and shoes, raisins, sugar and ginger. Clocks were made, books were bound. On the quays on both sides of the river, and especially on the Skeldergate side, there was a busy trade in wine and madder, alum, spices, grain, salt, wax, sea coal, steel, iron, linen and lead from the Yorkshire Dales (which became an increasingly important commodity in York and for which the city tried unsuccessfully at the end of the period to capture the staple).

But central to the economy of the city was the textile industry and that marked York's rise and decline. From the second half of the fourteenth century, weaving dominated the city's work; a sign of its growing significance was the number of new freemen drawn from that trade; they included weavers, drapers, dyers, fullers and shearmen. York was the centre of the trade and almost had a monopoly.

In the fifteenth century the trade declined. There were several reasons. Whereas the older mills worked happily on relatively sluggish water such as York's, the introduction of mechanized fulling processes led to the moving of the mills into the upper valleys where overshot wheels could take the place of the undershot wheels which were the only possible type in the lower vales. The guilds resisted the mechanization of the process and thus turned their backs on what has been described as the Industrial Revolution of the fourteenth century. Leeds, Wakefield and Halifax gained where York lost. There water power was easier, the weavers could keep their cows as well as their weaving sheds and fuel was cheaper. The wood that had been easily available in York was no longer so plentiful, as a survey of disforestation in 1549 confirms. For the other towns, but not for York, coal was cheaper.

Furthermore York declined as a port. From the fourteenth century onwards Hull began to rival it seriously. As Hull became a national port, York retreated to its status as a regional market. Its role as a centre for the export trade was in no way more magnificently demonstrated than in the foundation of the Guild of Merchant Adventurers, the basis of whose wealth was the export of woollen cloth and the centre of whose activities was the quayside, the river and the ships that lined it. Their guild was established in the middle of the fourteenth century when they were described as Mercers and Merchants; not until the fifteenth century did they become Adventurers. In their magnificent timbered hall on Fossgate at the heart of the commercial sector, they became a social club almost as soon as they became a thriving commercial group. Their attitudes were symptomatic. As other towns began to compete, some commented acidly that York's decline was as much its own fault as that of anyone else. York suffered—as to some extent it still does—from its own exclusiveness.

That criticism could be applied to other guilds and professional associations. In addition to the merchant guilds, York had by the middle of the fourteenth century about eighty craft guilds. They controlled work and set standards, fixed wages and prices and set the conditions for apprentices. They also operated as closed shops and their conservatism may have had a serious effect ultimately upon the activities of the city. More satisfying to the majority of citizens was their activity in organizing processions and plays. In particular, the Guild of Corpus Christi was responsible for the Mystery Plays. The York cycle contained forty-eight plays, which were presented in the streets for the Festival of Corpus Christi in May or June, starting at 4.30 in the morning and moving about throughout the day to the twelve stations where the plays were in turn performed, each by a different guild. They ceased after 1572 and only returned to the city after the Second World War.

The population of the mediaeval city reflects the economic changes. Its recovery from the devastation of the Conquest dates from the twelfth century. At the end of the eleventh the population was probably between 4,000 and 5,000; by the beginning of the fourteenth century it seems to have doubled, as people came in from the surrounding countryside. By the second half of the century it may have reached 11,000 and by its end about 13,000; some estimates put it as high as 14,000 or 15,000 Then it declined. By the end of the fifteenth century one estimate gives it as 7,000 and only 1,000 more in the early sixteenth century.

The decline was partly the result of economic recession, but it was also much affected by outbreaks of plague. The Black Death reached York in 1349 and lasted a year. There were further outbreaks in 1361, 1369, 1375, 1378 and 1391. Even in the sixteenth century there were bad years. Bubonic plague broke out in 1538 and again in 1550, especially west of the Ouse in the parish of St Martin-cum-Gregory. Constables were stationed on Ouse Bridge to prevent infected persons from crossing and infecting the east bank. Such precautions were taken on other occasions too. In 1563 there was an outbreak in London as a result of which Londoners were banned from the city of York unless they submitted to a period of quarantine. Four councillors who visited London despite the warnings were fined for their irresponsibility in doing so. By that time however the population had started to rise again. By the end of the period of this chapter it was more than 10,000 and was still rising.

Against that background of political, economic and social change, it is possible to view the physical elaboration of the city, and especially its major dominants.

If the castle and the markets were two of the definitive components of the mediaeval city, the third was without question the most splendid. The buildings and lands of the Church were developed throughout the period. There had already been a number of parish churches in the city before the Norman Conquest; in the thirteenth century many more were built; there was a slight pause during the fourteenth century, though by no means a complete one; and another wave of building in the fifteenth.

The parish churches of York have certain local characteristics but in the main conform to the national periods of mediaeval architecture. A selection of the more outstanding churches, approximately in their order of building, includes the sturdy and primitive St Mary Bishophill Junior, with its tower of herringbone masonry of the twelfth century, St John's Ousebridge of the twelfth, fourteenth and fifteenth centuries, the elegant, airy and soaring St Martin-cum-Gregory of the thirteenth to the fifteenth centuries but looking mainly fifteenth, All Saints North Street of the fourteenth and fifteenth centuries, with its celebrated stained glass, All Saints Pavement, also fourteenth to fifteenth centuries, with a beautiful octagonal stone lantern of top of its tower of the late fifteenth century, Holy Trinity Goodramgate of the same, with (a characteristically York feature) nave and aisles of the same height, St Mary Castlegate with its unusually tall fifteenth century octagonal tower and spire.

The churches were by no means the most spectacular buildings owned by the Church. The most extensive and comprehensive was St Mary's Abbey, taking the place of the former Earl's Palace in the precinct just outside the city walls known as Earlsborough in the tenth and eleventh centuries. The present ruins of the abbey church, evocative as they are, especially during performances of the Mystery Plays, give only a faint impression of the mediaeval splendour of the Abbey. Before 1086 Count Alan of Brittany had given St Olave's Church and four acres of land next to it to monks driven out of Whitby and Lastingham. That was the beginning of the richest and most impressive Benedictine house in the north of England. William Rufus enlarged the acreage of land and granted the Abbey a charter. The precinct when complete enclosed about twelve acres.

Like many other buildings in York—and like the defences—the abbey underwent a major reconstruction in the thirteenth century. The Norman church, erected in the eleventh century and damaged in the fire that swept across the city in 1137, was replaced. The new complex, dating from 1270 onwards, was elaborate and massive. From the west a gatehouse entered from Marygate; along the south the precinct fronted to the river. There was a half-timbered guest house on that side, conventual buildings to the east and in due course an abbot's house to the north. The Abbey church itself was an extraordinarily elaborate edifice for one so close to the Minster. It was 350 feet long, had an aisled nave and choir, transepts and a central tower with a spire. It was a complex as big and diversified as one of the major rural abbeys, with five or six quadrangles, occupying most of the present abbey gardens.

St Mary's was the grandest abbey. Further out, on Micklegate, was Holy Trinity priory, founded in the eleventh century, another Benedictine house, this one a daughter house of the Abbey of Marmoutier. More evenly spread over the city from the thirteenth century were the convents of the friars, whose preaching in the streets became an established feature of city life. There were Augustinians near the river by the later Guildhall, Franciscans near the castle, Dominicans just inside the city wall at Toft Green, Carmelites near the river Foss towards the east. There were also at one time seventeen hospitals and almshouses, though by 1500 eleven of them had already been converted to other uses. The major hospital, St Leonard's, beside the Abbey and the city wall, had 140 beds and was considered one of the largest hospitals in England. It was not alone. St Nicholas's Hospital looked after lepers. And near the Minster was a College for Chantry priests, erected in 1465, whose nocturnal activities are said to have lent some colour to the streets of York.

But looming over everything, growing bigger and grander with every century and eventually reducing everything else, even St Mary's Abbey, to relative insignificance, was the Minster. Over 500 feet long and 100 feet wide, with a central tower nearly 200 feet high, it was one of the largest of all the English cathedrals. It was rebuilt four times after the original building of a church for the baptism of King Edwin, taking the place of the Roman praetorium at the centre of the old Roman fortress; it was thus an example of the church's policy of Christianizing pagan locations and making of significant relics an even more significant Christian shrine. The Minster had been reorientated and placed correctly on the site, facing east and west, in the eighth century. The Church thus changed the sense of the city and the grain of its streets; for the rectilinear form of the old Roman camp and the streets within it was fundamentally disturbed—and disturbed moreover by what was now, in the early thirteenth century, the most dominant building in the city. The roads that could no longer go through the site or past it twisted and turned and joined the Danish tracks which had similarly altered the city's geometry. Monkgate, the city road leading to the north east, to Malton and Scarborough, was realigned to meet Goodramgate; Petergate, the original Via Principalis, began to waver and turn away a little from the Minster precinct.

The main part of the present Minster was begun in the thirteenth century. From that century date the transepts. The nave and choir are fourteenth century, the towers are fifteenth century. And there were many later additions. But the Minster essentially presents the image of such a building at the end of the mediaeval period; it was substantially complete by 1472.

Its recent cleaning suddenly revealed the grandeur of its interior as well as its exterior. The magnesian limestone glimmers in the sun and inside is streaked with colour when the sun shines through the stained glass windows. There are 117 windows and they contain nearly half the mediaeval stained glass in Britain. The Five Sisters, strange, mysterious tall lancets at the end of the north transept, are filled with grisaille glass of the thirteenth century and are probably the best known; but nothing excels the work of John Thornton in the great east window, completed in the fifteenth century, a supreme exercise of the glazier's art. Filled with scenes and episodes, it demonstrates the vision of the late mediaeval artist; its understanding requires not an instant but many protracted visits. Thornton, who came to York from Coventry in 1405, was one of the luminaries in a school of glass painters that gave York a national and international reputation.

If to imagine the castle as only Clifford's Tower is to misunderstand the nature and scope of the castle, the assumption that the present Minster represents the mediaeval one in its full meaning and presence is equally mistaken. The Minster itself was the soaring, spacious centrepiece of a complex of buildings and a society that was more than a physical entity. Its precinct was the home and the offices of the Archbishop, a potentate of wide social and political influence as well as spiritual authority, of canons, chantry priests and vicars choral. The Dean and Chapter owned and operated their own law courts, prisons and gallows (these in the place called Horsefair to the north of the walled city).

The Minster proper was thus a precinct that contained most of—and controlled all of— these multifarious activities. Stonegate, the line of the Roman Via Praetoria, narrowed at its head and after crossing Petergate became Minster Gates, a narrow bend leading into the Minster precinct. The precinct, with the huge bulk of the Minster squatting diagonally in the centre, was a grassed and cobbled enclosure interrupted by buildings and surrounded on most sides by houses and by a twelve-foot high wall.

A visitor exploring that precinct and moving through it clockwise after entering Minster Gates, would pass the church of St Michael-le-Belfrey, houses and offices occupied by canons and deacons, Peter's Prison and the huge sprawling Archbishop's Palace, huddling close to the north-west corner of the Minster and spreading backwards and across to the north with its cloisters, hall and chapel (now the Minster Library). Further to the north-east and east were more canons' houses, as there are today, and the house of the Treasurer (superseded by the later, existing, Treasurer's House), a college for chantry priests, St William's College, erected in the fifteenth century and Vicar's Lane (the present College Street) running past it. The lane went on through a timber roofed gate under a gallery, across Goodramgate and into the Bedern, to the chapel, hall and houses of the Vicars Choral. Further back and to the south was the Deanery. The whole precinct was thus radically unlike the present calm and ordered corner of the city; it was an informal assembly of variegated buildings of different dates, sizes and types, like a ramshackle university college dwarfed by an enormous church. On all sides, roads led from it into the city, with gates at Minster Gates, Lop Lane (at the west end of the Minster, beside Peter Prison), Ogleforth (behind St William's College) and the Bedern. To and from the Motte and the Minster and the Markets—the three determinants of the mediaeval city's form—the roads and footways needled their way, thrusting, twisting and turning through an increasingly tight huddle of houses and a multitude of workshops and churches and chapels. They retained, whenever possible, their ancient lines, spreading or narrowing a little as they approached their destination, sprouting new buildings in a constant state of adaptation and change.

The Danish route joining the main road from the south to the principal market area was Micklegate. Where it crossed the Ouse a timber bridge was built, which collapsed in 1154 under the weight of a crowd of foolhardy people gathered there to welcome the new Archbishop of York. The stone one which took its place in the thirteenth century was gradually lined with buildings until it became York's Rialto; at its busiest it had on it the Council Chamber, the Mayor's Parlour, a prison, a hospital, a chapel and twenty houses with shops on each side.

Foss Bridge was similarly crammed with buildings—but Ouse Bridge was the most strategically important. It led to the old market and to Castlegate and the gateway to the castle. From it branched off smaller and narrower roads (for Micklegate was the 'great' street) to various named precincts. On the right bank of the river it was crossed by Skeldergate with its wharves and the common crane on one side and North Street with its church and merchants' houses on the other. On the left bank, across the bridge, it branched off into many narrow roads, leading to markets and workshops.

But what, after all, was the city itself actually like? Looking at York today it is easy to mistake its appearance for that of a mediaeval city. The winding streets, the narrow alleys, the jettied houses, the stone walls around the edge of the central area invite visitors to mingle with history; but it is a history of subsequent changes as much as of the original place. The mediaeval city was a very different place at the end of the period from what it was at the beginning.

The city of the twelfth century was in ruins and little of it survives. Nor was that the last disaster. In 1137 a great fire swept through it again, demolishing many of the timber houses and the new churches. It was from that time onwards that the city began to take on a new distinctive shape. And particularly in the thirteenth century; for that was when the majority of the religious houses were built, when the hospitals were founded, when the Minster and the huge Abbey were rebuilt as well, when the city walls were topped out in stone and the castle was given new defences and a new shell keep at the top, when the bridges over the Ouse and the Foss were made of stone and when houses began to be built on them. There are plenty of references to poor streets and poor paving, but generally, with all that freshly quarried magnesian limestone looking so sunny and clean, with new houses along the streets, still mainly of timber, punctuated occasionally by grander stone dwellings like the Norman house at the top of Stonegate, the city must have looked picturesque and cheerful.

There is another respect in which it is difficult to visualize accurately the mediaeval city. It was a place of zealously guarded ownerships and heavily defined boundaries. With the Abbey, the priories, the Minster, the friaries, the hospitals, the castle, as well as the posterns and bars, the whole city must have presented a constant picture of walls. For all of these places had enclosures and all had walls. There were walls—mostly stone walls—everywhere. Along Lendal and Toft Green, St Saviourgate and Castlegate, the walls of the friaries lined the edges and were punctuated only by locked gates. In the smarter districts everything must have seemed very private. And indeed it was; it was a later fashion to open everything up.

At the edge of the walled town the great Forest of Galtres stretched away to the north. It was a royal demesne, which had been a favourite hunting ground of the Saxon kings; it stretched some 20 miles from York to Aldborough. It was a hunting district. Some idea of its complexity can be gained from the fact that in the fourteenth century not only did it contain about 100,000 acres but also about sixty townships. Its boundary line, which was checked in 1316, began at the 'foot of the wall of the city of York', ran north to Crayke and thence by Stillington, to Strensall and Huntingdon to join the city wall again at Layerthorpe Bridge. It was a forest of oak and birch and alder, with dense thickets and swampy patches, with rushes and reeds. In it were wild boars and red deer and birds of prey—buzzards and harriers.

If that forest reached down to touch the city on the north, the four strays, or common pasture lands, touched both that and its other sides. Now more than 800 acres in extent, the strays are the residue of much more extensive areas of common land—Micklegate Stray (now mainly occupied by the racecourse) on the south-west, Bootham Stray on the north, Monk Stray towards the north-east, and Walmgate Stray to the south-east. They were enclosed at the end of the eighteenth century and taken over by the Corporation in the twentieth.

In that landscape, constantly being adjusted throughout the Middle Ages, the city stood sturdy and self-confident. For as it reached the climax of its fortunes in the fourteenth century it began to explode and erupt in interesting ways. The Minster got bigger and bigger, higher and higher. New institutions, like the Merchant Adventurers whose Hall was built in 1357, joined the building boom. All the churches were recast. By the fifteenth century towers and spires were appearing on most of them. New houses lined the streets, like Lady Row in Goodramgate, a two-storey jettied terrace just outside the churchyard of Holy Trinity, erected about 1320, or the later half-timbered houses in Micklegate,

Stonegate and North Street beside the Church of All Saints. They were still relatively low, plainer than in some other towns, leaning over the edge of the street, in some cases—as still in the Shambles—almost joining across it.

Around the markets houses crowded tightly with their ground floors opened up as shops, with benches and trestles for displaying goods. Near the river, the water lanes sliced down to the quayside near the Franciscan Friary; down at that quayside there were sailing ships and other boats. On the other side the quay was just as busy. A substantial river wall had been built in 1305 and warehouses began to line the staith by the end of the Middle Ages. At high tide it must all have looked very cheerful; at low tide the black mud of the river banks—as well as its smell—must have given a more macabre impression.

Above all there were two characteristics which are not obvious today. The first was that by the fourteenth century the development in the centre exploded outside the walls as well. There were houses outside Bootham Bar, Micklegate Bar and Monk Bar, near Skeldergate Postern and Gillygate; the Jews had moved to a suburb just outside the walls on the north-east. And there were constant disputes—the Council trying to force people to clear out of the defences and out of the ditch, citizens deploring the attitude of the Council as volubly as they do today.

The second was the way in which the land was used. In that 263 acres inside the walls there were for most of the time only about 10,000 people. It was fairly dense, of the order of 40 people per acre and must have been crowded. But not in the way the central area seems today. The mediaeval city was a city of narrow lanes and houses crowded on to them, of jettied buildings with attics and cellars, some developed at right angles to the streets along lanes leading into yards. But behind those blocks of houses was a great deal of open space, with orchards and gardens and farmyards. The religious houses presumably had both, and their gardens must have acted as lungs, with trees and shrubs and grass and birds. But probably much the most obtrusive, in smell as well as in noise and appearance, were the yards. Especially those with pigs.

York has always had a reputation for bad smells. Edward III thought it one of the most disgusting places in the kingdom. Part of the reason for that was the constant presence of butchers' offal rotting in the streets or the ditches. It was not the only refuse. Privies were built on the edge of the city moat as well as on Ouse Bridge. A description of the fifteenth century refers to the city's 'great corruptions and horrible and pernicious air'. And all the efforts of reformers do not seem to have had much effect. They scored small victories. In 1482 an order was passed banishing prostitutes to the suburbs, as if the suburbs were in some way a more appropriate beat; in 1549 an order was passed to destroy pigsties; at innumerable times in the fifteenth century attempts were made to improve the water supply. But the general impression remains—of foul and littered streets, of uncollected garbage, of dogs and cats and rats skulking along the battered walls, of mice and lice, of chickens clucking and dogs barking and crows shrieking and horses neighing—and always people pursuing pigs down the streets trying to get them out of the way or locked up in back yards. It was a small and smelly and very noisy northern capital.

And yet, despite all that, it was known to be splendid and beautiful. How rich it was in monuments; how gaily decorated; how richly furnished its houses and churches; how competent the pottery and metal work, the clothes and pictures and tapestries. There were such elegant buildings—the Guildhall, the Merchant Adventurers', St Anthony's Hall, St William's College, the priories and friaries and churches, the almshouses and hospitals. And over it all was the Minster, its three great towers reaching up in the fifteenth century, its stained glass, with that of many of the parish churches, making York one of the great centres of the arts and crafts in England and indeed in Europe. It had lost its library at the time of the Conquest. It had now a stature as an artistic centre that made it enviable.

It was the second biggest city in the kingdom. It had superlative walls, four great gates, a castle, a cathedral, an abbey, a priory and a major hospital; it had four friaries, thirty one churches and eight smaller hospitals inside the walls, and nine churches, five chapels, seven hospitals, a nunnery and a priory outside the walls; it had a guildhall, two great merchants' halls, a council chamber and chapel and other crowded buildings on its central bridge. In a landscape of timber and brick and thatch, the white and honey-coloured limestone of the major buildings glittered and sparkled. To the stranger approaching from the south following the old Roman route through Tadcaster and seeing Micklegate Bar from the top of the hill, it was a pageant of spires and pinnacles and towers; inside the Bar the road wound down between walls, the corners punctuated with churches; it was a city not just of markets or of religious or of lords, it was a city of style and splendour.

Now that city was to experience another destruction, almost as great as that which initiated the period. The end of this chapter has to be the event which fundamentally transformed it again. That was not the death of a king or the end of a royal dynasty; it was the destruction of the organization which effectively dictated the shape of the city.

With the suppression of the monasteries in 1536 and 1539, the city of York was torn apart once again. Within a few years the huge Abbey of St Mary's was a quarry, the priories were eliminated, the churches reduced. But the dissolution of the monasteries meant more than a religious change; it was a change of the most profound economic significance. It provoked what was possibly the last of the great popular risings in England—the Pilgrimage of Grace of 1536, one of the most moving and tragic of the events of the Tudor reigns.

It nearly succeeded; but the pilgrims, persuaded by false assurances, disbanded and were relentlessly betrayed. Their leader, Robert Aske, who had entered York at the head of between 20,000 and 40,000 pilgrims and prayed in the Minster, was condemned to death and hung alive in chains from the top of Clifford's Tower. He took more than a week dying and his body hung there for more than a year.

With that episode the story of mediaeval York comes to a grisly close. As the city shook itself into another posture, it still huddled around the castle and Clifford's Tower. The castle thus serves as the symbol of the end of the period as well as of its beginning. But now it is not a motte being hurriedly fortified and enclosed; it is a crumbling, obsolete stone keep and a decaying body dangling in chains from its parapet—a tribute to the failure of popular protest against power.

4. The King's Manor

The biggest change in the face of the city since its destruction in 1069 was caused by the dissolution of the monasteries—the smaller ones in 1536, the larger ones in 1539. The city that had crowded round a major Benedictine abbey, other monasteries both inside and outside the walls, four friaries and forty parish churches was fundamentally disrupted. This time it was not a single cataclysm but a succession of such events. Within five years the religious houses were in ruins, the parish churches were reduced and reorganized, the hospitals were derelict and—more lastingly effective if at first only indicated by the visible ruins of the old order—new forces and ownerships were in existence that would in time transform the city and give it a different social and economic character.

York probably looked its best at the time of the accession of Henry VIII; it probably looked its worst by the end of the century. By that time more than ten parish churches had been shut down as well as all the religious houses; St William's Chapel on Ouse Bridge had been turned into a bourse or exchequer for the merchants; the great hospital of St Leonards was in ruins.

In that respect the Reformation was an economic disaster for York. The translation of the abbeys and priories into stone quarries, and the throwing of their land upon the market caused a slump in land values. Some individuals did very well out of it, taking over the lands of the abbeys outside York as well as within it; the majority came off very badly. The Pilgrimage of Grace, that ended the last chapter, was thus a protest that arose not just from religious but from social and economic grievances. The disappearance of the religious houses was attended by unemployment as well as the almost total disappearance of the trades and crafts associated with them. Stained glass, for example, which had been one of the glories of York in the fifteenth century, declined into insignificance and then came to an end. The last of the glass painters in that tradition, Henry Gyles, died in 1709 a poor man. The Festivals gradually wound down or were wound up. With the end of the Corpus Christi Guild in 1546 the Festival organized by that Guild on the day of the feast gradually ceased—and with it the Mystery Plays, the last performance of one of them being in 1572. For that reason alone York must have been a sadder place at the end of the century than at the beginning.

For the monasteries played a fundamental part in the economy of the country. In Yorkshire the great abbeys were also the greatest owners of agricultural land. Rievaulx and Byland to the north, Fountains and Jervaulx to the west, Selby to the south and Kirkham Priory to the east literally surrounded York with their lands. The protests of the Pilgrims in 1536 had therefore many targets—the enclosure of land by the new landowners: the elimination of the monasteries as shelter for travellers and homes for the old and poor: the feeling that with the change in the old order the north was even more subject to the south and the growing power of central government.

The revolution in the environment of the city was ultimately brought about because the abbeys and priories were worth raiding. In the tasteless scrabble that followed the passing of the Acts for the dissolution of the monasteries, it was not only a few parvenus who obtained their land; more or less everyone joined in the search for loot—for stone and doors and windows and bells and screens and wood and lead. At least until the building of a few great houses in the city, which did not occur until the end of the century, York must have looked like a place plundered by new conquerors. The abbeys and priories had occupied a major portion of the land inside the walls; for the moment that property lay derelict and the people who might have lived there joined the growing numbers of the poor for whom provision had ultimately to be made.

Out of the ruins emerged the building that forms the title of this chapter, the hub of the life of the city in the period from the dissolution of the monasteries to the end of the Civil War just over a hundred years later. That is the King's Manor, now part of the University of York.

When the last Abbot of St Mary's, with his fifty monks, handed over the Abbey to the King in 1539, its handsome land and gardens, occupying twelve acres just outside the city wall, itself enclosed in a wall built about 1266, contained not only a ruined church and monastic buildings; it offered also the capacious Abbot's House, parts of it dating from the thirteenth century, most of it from the abbacy of William Sever at the end of the fifteenth century.

With a gateway to Bootham, made by Sever, the U-shaped building of brick and stone, two storeys with an open court facing towards the south-west, was ideally suited to become the offices for the King's Council in the North and then a residence for the Lord President of the Council. The additions and alterations, which make it today one of the most fascinating historic buildings in the country as well as one of the most difficult to interpret, were the work of successive Lords President, making it more convenient as a dwelling and as the headquarters of government in the north of England.

The King's Council in the North was set up in the first instance by Richard III. It was one of two—the equivalent in the west being the Council for Wales, situated in Ludlow. It was used only slightly by Henry VII, re-established by Henry VIII in 1522 (under the Duke of Richmond who lived in Sheriff Hutton castle north-east of the city) and reorganized again in 1530 and 1533. Its existence and function remain shadowy until after that time and specifically until after the Pilgrimage of Grace, several of whose leaders were members of the Council. With the failure of the Pilgrimage and the removal of its leaders, the Council was re-established once again. Its head however was no longer simply the King's Lieutenant in the North; he was now designated Lord President of the Council and was instructed to take up residence in York. The first active President was Robert Holgate who took up office in 1538; coming from Llandaff and having no house in York until he became Archbishop in 1545, he was given the Abbot's House immediately after the suppression of the Abbey in 1539.

The Abbey Precinct was impeccably situated for the purpose. It was close to all the main functions of the city, but was legally no part of it, being outside the city walls but within its own. As such it could avoid conflict with the jurisdiction of the city; and since the jurisdiction of the city was complicated enough, and the authority of the various bodies —the Mayor and Council, the Church, the Courts and the Council in the North itself— must have overlapped, it was a sensible location.

The Council was essentially a legal body, a replacement for the incessantly travelling Courts of the Middle Ages. It had three main areas of concern—the bringing of criminals to justice, the hearing of cases about debts and other civil offences, and the enforcing of religious observance. At a period when the rest of government did not closely affect the common man, it was therefore in effect the supreme executive authority north of the Trent and the main medium of communication between central government and the King's northern subjects; it became an integral part of the constitution of the country. Its authority extended over Yorkshire, Durham, Northumberland, Westmorland and Cumberland and included the cities and towns of York, Carlisle, Hull and Berwick. It had a staff of over 300 officials. About 450 lawsuits were brought to it each year, involving over 2,000 suitors. With accompanying people as well, it meant unprecedented crowds of visitors, staying in the many new inns which were opened. In effect it made York the capital of the North of England for just over 100 years. Its loss, just before the Civil War, when, in King Charles I's words, it was 'shaken into pieces rather than dissolved', was keenly felt. After 1660 the citizens petitioned for its restoration—unsuccessfully.

The most notable figures in its history were Holgate (Lord President from 1538 to 1550), Sir Thomas Gargrave (Vice President from 1555 to 1579), the Earl of Huntingdon

(Lord President from 1572 to 1595), Lord Sheffield (Lord President from 1603 to 1619) and the unfortunate Wentworth, Earl of Strafford (Lord President from 1628 to 1641 though non-resident after 1633). Under them the Manor was spasmodically and rather oddly transformed into a rambling set of offices and rooms and public chambers which have made it easily adaptable for widely different uses ever since. To the refaced and reorganized Abbot's House was added a suite of rooms and a council chamber with an elaborate decorative frieze in the time of Huntingdon, a new Dining Hall and a single storey gallery forming an enclosed court in the time of Sheffield and another floor, a handsome new stairway to the Council Chamber and carved coats of arms (one of which features in his articles of impeachment) in the time of Wentworth. Together with a range of cellars further west, roughly on the line of the monastic east range, reputedly erected for the visit of Henry VIII in 1541 and topped by two more floors of rooms, the whole site became a complex of government and residential buildings and the hub of the city and the region.

As people poured in, the King's Manor gave a character to York that it did not have before and never had again. The golden age of the Council in the North has always been said to have been during the presidency of Henry Hastings, Earl of Huntingdon, when the buildings certainly took on a new splendour. Known as the Puritan Earl, he succeeded in enforcing some law and order in the north—an effective, if not for everyone a very attractive man. The Jesuit Father Richard Holtby, writing an account of persecution in the north in 1593, described him as a man 'of bloody and cruel mind against Catholic men and their religion; and one, as he is thought, of no deep reach in matters of weight and judgement, yet through continual practice in persecuting us these twenty-two years he has borne the office of President, is grown so ingenious to work us trouble and disquietness, that herein he need not give place unto any, though they be of greater wit and capacity...'

Huntingdon was at least successful. The last of the Lords President was not. Wentworth pursued his famous policy of 'thorough' without an appropriate master for such a policy. His ability was recognized and feared—and his overbearing personality won him many enemies. The corridors of the Manor are said to be haunted by his ghost.

The King's Manor was not the only major architectural achievement of the age. But it was symptomatic. In place of the abbeys and priories, the Tudor and Jacobean periods saw the foundation of a number of mansions, predecessors of the out-of-town mansions that followed in the next century. The four main mansions in York were the King's Manor itself, the Duke of Buckingham's House in the parish of Bishophill Senior, an extensive brick building with elaborate gables, demolished in the eighteenth century, the Treasurer's House, a private house built about 1600 on the site of the mediaeval treasurer's dwelling, updated in the eighteenth century and now the property of the National Trust, and Sir Arthur Ingram's house, no longer in existence, which occupied the site of the present Purey Cust Nursing Home to the west of the Minster.

The story of that house is as symbolic as that of the King's Manor and throws light on the Church as the latter does on the Crown. Until the Reformation the ground to the immediate west and north of the Minster was occupied by the Archbishop's Palace, a capacious and spreadeagled range of buildings that were offices as well as house. Of that palace only the chapel (now the Minster Library) and a fragment of a twelfth century arcade remain today. Its destruction started under Archbishop Young, Archbishop from 1561 to 1568 and President of the Council from 1564, who endowed his son with a legacy by selling the lead from the roof of the palace. The palace thus ceased to be habitable and in 1570 the succeeding Archbishop moved a few miles downstream to Bishopthorpe. Incredible as it now seems, about 1616 the ruins and the land were sold to Sir Arthur Ingram, who built a new house near the north-west corner of the nave of the Minster and laid out pleasure gardens, with statues, a tennis court, an orchard, a bowling green, walks and fishponds in the north-west angle of the city walls. The mansion was one of the sights of York. Charles I stayed there in 1642.

The splendour of those few mansions in no way compensated for the general decline of the city's wealth and the poverty of a large proportion of the inhabitants. The decline of the wool trade, discussed in the last chapter, continued. Halifax, Leeds and Wakefield, better placed for water supplies and energy, took over increasingly, and the development of Hull as a port almost wholly displaced York as a harbour. Fuel problems became worse. The Forest of Galtres, so long a source of timber and fuel, had receded to between twenty and thirty miles from York by the sixteenth century and was almost wholly cleared in the seventeenth. And on top of that a series of disastrous plagues, ultimately attributed to the growing foulness of the water supply, wrecked the prosperity and confidence of the city. There were plagues in 1538, 1550, 1552, 1570, 1579, 1604, 1631 and later. Though the Council of the North contributed money towards improving the water supply, it was a long time before anything was done.

By the time of Charles I, as the Recorder of York declared in a speech to the King, the river had become partially blocked. York, he said, had no hope of its 'former splendour and greatness' if the river was not 'made serviceable'; and he gave a long account of how the river up to and above York could be used for trade in lead, flax, butter, cheese, hams, tallow, hose for the army and timber for the navy. His plea was not answered.

The population remained stationary in the sixteenth century but increased in the early seventeenth. It was about 10,000 in 1600 and increased to about 12,000 by 1630 when York was still the second city in the country, rivalled only by Bristol, Norwich and Exeter. From then the population seems to have remained stationary until the end of the century. It is therefore not surprising that relatively little ordinary housing and development seems to have taken place. There were the new almshouses, five built in the seventeenth century, two of which remain today—Ingram's Almshouses in Bootham of about

1640 and Ann Middleton's in Skeldergate of about 1659, later rebuilt when the road was widened. There was one new and admirable church, St Michael le Belfrey of 1525–37, close beside the Minster. There was a certain amount of ordinary rebuilding in existing streets, in Stonegate, Petergate, Shambles and Fossgate, there crowding the entrance to the late mediaeval Merchant Adventurers' Hall. Of the street houses the best is the Herbert House in Pavement. Of the streets none looks now as it did in the period. The best impression of a seventeenth century street in York is probably gained from the Shambles, the mediaeval butchers' street; despite modern restoration of individual buildings, the overall shape of the street and most of the houses are basically as they appeared about the time of the Civil War.

Apart from that, there were gardens, orchards, jettied houses, mostly half timbered in the earlier part of the century, increasingly built of brick in the latter half of it in answer to constant fire hazards and the passing of regulations to prevent fire. Warehouses lined the quays; forges, smithies and inns were everywhere. From its mediaeval shape the city did not change much and certainly did not improve. Refuse lay around the streets and lined the river banks. Street lighting, with lamps on groups of houses, was tried out in the 1580s; otherwise it was dark and dangerous. The water supply was unsatisfactory, the air, as many people reported, bad, and the ubiquitous pigs kept on squealing in the streets.

The most spectacular and romantic of the new structures was Ouse Bridge. Over the years it had become crowded not with people but with buildings, as also had Foss Bridge, of which a writer remarked that by the end of the sixteenth century you could not tell when you were on it. In addition to the houses and shops, Ouse Bridge supported St William's Chapel at one end, transformed into an exchequer and later into apartments after the Reformation. In 1564, after snow, a frost, a sudden thaw and a rise in the river, the two central arches collapsed. Twelve houses and twelve people fell into the river and the people were drowned. It took two years to start repairs and a good deal of argument, especially about money; in the end, whoever paid for the building, the rents from the shops paid for its maintenance. The bridge that replaced the old one after 1566 was one of the sights of the city. Still topped with buildings and the chapel (now a council chamber), a Sunday school, courts and a prison beneath in what must have been the dampest situation in the country, it had five arches of which the centre one, popular with artists and engravers until its demolition in 1810, was 81 feet wide and over 17 feet high. The gradients were fierce and the road narrow. But it was crucial to the city; for Ouse Bridge was the only link between the two parts of the city and a centre for social life and trade.

It is from this time that the first useful map of York dates. That is John Speed's map of the West Riding of Yorkshire of 1610, which has an inset plan of YORKE. The walls are more or less as they were in the Middle Ages and still are except for the breach in them at St Leonards. The main streets are crowded with houses, the back lands free and open.

The old Via Principalis—Petergate, Fossgate and Walmgate—curving to the south to cross the Foss, seems the most strongly marked street, running north-west to south-east. There are roads all around the walls except for the portion near the Fishponds between Walmgate Bar and Layerthorpe Postern, and houses outside the walls along the main roads. On Blossom Street, the road to London, they line both sides and turn the corner outside Micklegate Bar. They line Bootham and Marygate, run down one side of Gillygate, along both sides of Monkgate, around Layerthorpe Bridge and outside Walmgate Bar.

What is even more striking is the number of windmills on all sides of the city not far from the walls. Speed's map shows no less than eleven and he makes a major feature of them. They must have made a significant difference to the aspect of the city in the seventeenth century. The view by William Lodge (in the City Art Gallery) taken from Windmill Rise on the London road about 1680 shows York surrounded by its stone city wall, running straight across the painting, with a few buildings outside it and a few clumps of trees. The Minster, the castle and a few spires rise about the level of the walls. In the foreground are the sails of a windmill. Since York could not provide water power for many corn mills and since the main one was in any case the King's, it was logical that mills should be set up around the city. There in Lodge's view is York—a small, tatty, semi-derelict northern city with a smart wall around it, a few sprawling manors inside it and a lot of windmills in the fields outside.

The end of this period can conveniently be marked by the Civil War in which York featured for the last time as a military headquarters and a fortress. The castle was obsolete and already partially in decay; it needed only the explosion of a gun on the ramparts during a salute in 1684 to complete its gutting as dwelling and fort.

York's significance during the war was partly because of the importance of the city itself, but more because of the King's Manor. Charles I having moved his court to York for six months in 1642, the city became a headquarters for the King. By that time Wentworth had left York to face trial in London. Under a Bill of Attainder, he was executed in 1641, abandoned by the king he had too rigorously served.

The Civil War broke out in August 1642 in Nottingham. York's subsequent part in it was the direct result of the pact between Parliament and the Scots—the Solemn League and Covenant of 1644. In that year York was besieged by three armies. Following an explosion in the corner tower of the precinct wall, the King's Manor was invaded and the occupiers only driven out with difficulty. After a brilliant piece of marching and counter-marching, Prince Rupert advanced upon York and the besieging armies in an attempt to raise the siege. At the Battle of Marston Moor west of York the Royalists were disastrously defeated by the Scots under Leslie and the highly disciplined Ironsides under Cromwell. In July the city surrendered and never engaged in warfare again.

The last moments of the political significance of York might be taken as the long line of defeated soldiers scrambling back to Micklegate Bar and seeking shelter. The political supremacy of the city was a short and never very convincing episode. York was remote. A farm labourer, for example, working on the field at Marston Moor on the morning of the battle was cleared off the field by a patrol who told him that the King and Parliament were about to fight a battle there. 'What?', said he. 'Has them two fallen out then?'

His ignorance was symptomatic. The city retreated into itself. A few years later, Sir Thomas Widdrington, the Recorder of York, who had managed to keep in with all sides during and after the war, assembled a substantial collection of historical notes under the title *Analecta Eboracensia*. Having completed his massive book, he sent it with a proposed dedication to the Lord Mayor, Aldermen, Sheriffs, Common Council and Citizens about 1662. The reply he received incensed him sufficiently to forbid the publication of the work, which was however used by the historian Francis Drake in the next century and was published finally in 1897. That reply says so much about the state of the city and the state of mind of its leaders after the Restoration that quotations from it are used to close this chapter.

'Sir, You have told us by the former discourse what the city was and what our predecessors have been. We know not what this may have of honour in it: sure we are, it hath but little of comfort. The shoes of our predecessors are too big for our feet, and the ornaments which they had will not serve now to cover our nakedness, nor will their wealth feed us, who are not able to tell you what we are unless it be this, that we are poor and miserable . . . The inhabitants have many of them forsaken it, and those who have not, she cannot maintain, whilst some cities are become so big with buildings, and numerous with inhabitants, as they can be hardly fed or governed. York is left alone, situate in a country plentiful for provisions, and stored, if the people had money to buy them. Trade is decayed, the river become unnavigable by reason of shelves. Leeds is nearer the manufactures, and Hull more commodious for the vending of them; so York is, in each respect, furthest from the profit. . . As for our wealth, it is reduced to a narrow scantling; if we look upon the fabric and materials of the city, we have lost the suburbs which were our skirts, our whole body is in weakness and distemper, our merchandize and trade, our nerves and sinews, are weakened and become very mean and inconsiderable: . . . Now for all the monuments of our former state and glory we find no warmth or comfort from them; but it seems to add to our unhappiness that our predecessors were so happy. Give us leave for conclusion to tell you that a good purse is more useful to us than a long story, which might enable us: (1) to make our river more navigable; (2) to re-edify the decayed parts of the city; (3) to raise a stock to set up some manufacture in the city; (4) to relieve our poor, into which number we may all of us fall if some timely course be not taken by which, through God's blessing, this tottering and wasted city may be upheld.'

5. The Assembly Rooms

The Civil War was a turning point for York. The era that followed gave it a new character and added another—and permanent—dimension to its life and its position in the national scene. For nearly two centuries after the Restoration, York became a centre of fashion—with all that it implied not just for the fashionable people themselves but for those whose role it was to support them.

In terms of population it hardly grew. That of the eighteenth century changed little from that of the seventeenth. In the eighteenth century there were about 12,000 inhabitants for the first sixty years. Then, about 1760, the population began to increase and reached between 16,000 and 17,000 in 1800—it was 16,846 in the census of 1801. In that early limitation of increase the generally low health and early mortality of the people played a part; there were several exceptionally bad winters during the first half of the century and a series of epidemics and fevers.

It may even be that the habit of York's citizens, several times commented upon, of eating and drinking to excess, contributed to the high mortality rate. It is certainly the case that, as with most cities and towns in England, the population began to rise in the latter half of the century; for that was the time when the Enclosure Acts followed one another, the land was reorganized and regrouped, the old farming communities were broken up and the open-field system changed to one of closed fields, when pasture gave way in many areas to arable farming—and when—as a result of it all—people moved into new farm buildings or new villages or migrated to the towns. Of the human misery that accompanied that rural revolution and the urban revolution that was to boil over in the nineteenth century into the Industrial Revolution, enough has been written. For the sake of clarifying the role of a city such as York in the midst of it, it is however worth looking at the context of the city and at the factors that were effectively to transform it.

The Assembly Rooms

The change in farming patterns was already clear in the seventeenth century. Even at that time, most of England was still uncultivated and the possibilities of change must have been obvious. The process of change in ownership and farming methods, started at the Reformation and set back by the Civil War, could now be accelerated and seen in its reality. The unexploited and untreated land required capital and new techniques. The change of emphasis from pasture to arable farming made use of that land. It also reflected the fact that the price of wool had fallen, whereas the price of wheat and rye had risen. And that owed much to the contemporary development and growth of the towns, with populations needing food for themselves and for their animals. London's population rose to 900,000 at the end of the century. By that time the chief towns, those with a population exceeding 50,000, were no longer York and Norwich; they were Birmingham, Bristol, Leeds, Liverpool and Manchester. York, with less than 17,000, was well down the list.

In 1700 over half of the arable land in the country was organized on the communal open-field system. Enclosures on a big scale started in the middle of the century, even though a major belt of land in the north had already been enclosed; most of those affecting the north dated from about 1750, before the General Enclosure Act of 1801. Whereas in Scotland it was possible to enclose land with the minimum of administrative fuss and without special legislation, in England all enclosures until the General Enclosure Act required a special Act of Parliament. They reached a climax during the reign of George III, 1760–1820. On the estates surrounding York enclosures took place precisely in those years. The Vale of York became an area of wheat and barley. The great Forest of Galtres, after suffering during the Civil War, was already denuded in great part. Now hedges were planted, roads made, the land drained and small canals dug.

Within a ten-mile radius of York there are more than a hundred villages and hamlets, many of them dating from Anglo-Saxon and Danish times. But it was during this great agrarian revolution that most of them began to take on the character that they still have today. Their older and more significant houses date mainly from the eighteenth or nineteenth centuries, made of local bricks and roofed with local timber. This is the basic house which establishes the scale and form of the village, with a room on each side of a passage, bedrooms upstairs, sheds and a privy outside, usually but not invariably moved inside, and stone flagged floors now usually covered with asphalt.

The enclosure of farming land was only one aspect of the transformation of the countryside. Just as significant was the opening up of communications, making possible the transportation of goods and people which was an essential prerequisite for the Industrial Revolution.

The road system laid down in the Middle Ages still survived, suitable for local journeys but not for longer ones. Before the development of a national road system, it was the invention of the turnpikes at the end of the seventeenth century and throughout the eighteenth century which revolutionized travelling. Unsatisfactory as many of them were, they still constituted a notable improvement on the old local roads and the 'commutation' roads, for which labour had been commuted for a payment. In contrast to them, the turnpikes were financed by payment for use. As they quickly covered the country, their gates and toll houses began to provide punctuation points in the landscape. Of those surrounding York, a much admired turnpike was that to Thirsk, Easingwold and Northallerton, whose tollhouse just outside York still marks the entry to the village of Skelton.

Just as heavily used and a feature of the countryside were the drove roads. They were not just green ways or bridle ways used by packmen; they accommodated huge numbers of cattle and led to one of the most characteristic features of English roads—the wide grass margins in rural districts used by the cattle for grazing as they moved slowly along. As in many districts farming changed from pasture to arable, cattle rearing became more localized. Scotland, for example, sent huge herds to the markets in England. Between August 1777 and August 1778 no less that 28,551 cattle passed over Wetherby Bridge on the Great North Road 12 miles west of York.

But the most spectacular development was the making of the canals. The canals opened up new communications; their construction also involved the draining of land and its transformation for other purposes. The waterways that most affected York were to the east, based upon the Humber and the drainage of the flat land south of it— Hatfield Chase, the scene of King Edwin's last battle in 632. In the seventeenth century that land was drained by the Dutch canal expert Vermuyden, who laid out the straight stretch known as the Dutch River. In 1698 the Aire and Calder Navigation Company was formed. That led directly to the building of the new town of Goole at the end of the Dutch River.

By the early nineteenth century Goole was a focus for foreign trade; but already during the eighteenth century the estuary of the Humber had made links with unexpected regions of the country and become an outlet for goods on a significant scale. The connection of the Humber with the Trent and its subsidiary canals, and with the Aire and Calder Navigation, meant that a system of usable waterways connected the mouth of the Humber with the industrial West Riding of Yorkshire (and ultimately at the end of the eighteenth century, through the Pennines, with Liverpool), with the Midlands and as far as Shropshire.

York was profoundly affected. For York did not share in the major benefits of the innovation. Despite efforts throughout the eighteenth century, and the establishment of the Ouse Navigation in 1727, York remained isolated from the canal system. Traffic moving up the Ouse tended to stop at Selby and take to horses and go overland. And when in 1757 a lock was built at Naburn four miles downstream from the city in an attempt to improve the system it had the opposite effect. Industry and trade moved to other towns, especially those whose water supply had already robbed York of the most profitable parts of the woollen industry. York, in short, was no longer a centre of trade; its merchant adventurers were still eating and drinking, possibly even more than in the past, but they were adventuring no longer.

And that was entirely in keeping with the other major change in the surrounding landscape. The end of the Civil War, the changes in land use, the founding of new fortunes, often associated with the colonies, the prospects of peace and the restoration of the monarchy all contributed to the prosperity and style of the county families and the building of great country houses. What emerged in the eighteenth century was not just a new landscape of work and settlement, but a landscape of gentility and wealth.

In that explosion of building no factor was scenically more important than the recent knowledge of how to control the supply of water, the same science that led to the building of the canals. The control of water supplies meant that wealthy landowners could now erect their mansions on eminences and hills rather than in valley bottoms where the natural supply of water had previously confined them. It also meant that a mansion acquired a new character as a scenic dominant and that the whole of its surrounding land could be manipulated to provide an appropriate setting—ultimately the English park and the English picturesque.

The details of that movement do not concern this study. What does concern it is the concentration of country houses around the city of York and their effect on the city itself. Already, in the sixteenth and seventeenth centuries, there were mansions such as Temple Newsam near Leeds and Beningborough near York. Especially significant in the early years of this period was the building of three mansions in the most fashionable manner. They were Middlethorpe Hall at Bishopthorpe from 1699–1701, Castle Howard (the seat of the Earl of Carlisle) north-east of York by Sir John Vanburgh from 1699 and Bramham (the seat of Robert Benson, later Lord Bingley and Lord Mayor of York) south-west of the city from 1700 to 1710. Their example was followed in the next fifty years by almost everyone. The thirty miles surrounding York is as littered with country houses as it was in the later Middle Ages with religious houses—in some cases their sites coinciding and recording the origin of the family's fortunes. There are at least forty worth seeing today, and if the minor manors and granges are added, the number is formidable.

Their building made a major impact on the city. Benson, the owner (and possibly the architect) of Bramham Park, was Lord Mayor of York in 1707 as well as a Member of Parliament. His involvement in the city's affairs was in no way unusual. Until the coming of the railways, London was not the town centre for the families of the landed gentry for greater parts of the year. The social centre was the local town and especially an elegant one like York, already the seat of an archbishop, the site of the Assize Courts and a centre for racing. York became, in the phrase used by Daniel Defoe, the scene of 'the confluence of the gentry'.

Defoe made his tour through the 'Whole Island of Great Britain' between 1722 and 1724, half a century before the Industrial Revolution. But it was a country already in the midst of drastic change and the start of its emergence as a mercantile giant. He records the solidity and stability of the landed classes, but also the growing significance of the commercial families rapidly rising to positions of wealth and power and in Britain, if in no other country, combining through marriage with the older landed families.

His passages on York give as clear a picture of the city of his time as it is possible to obtain. He saw it in change. 'York is indeed a pleasant and beautiful city, and not at all the less beautiful for the works and lines about it being demolished, and the city, as it may be said, being laid open. For the beauty of peace is seen in the rubbish; the lines and bastions and demolished fortifications, have a reserved secret pleasantness in them from the contemplation of the publick tranquillity, that outshines all the beauty of advanced bastions, batteries, cavaliers, and all the hard named works of the engineers about a city.' He records the dereliction of the castle and in contrast the emergence of the bridge, the greatest arch in England, as a symbol of the 'risen' city; he finds York Minster 'the beautifullest church of the old building that is in Britain'; and reflects whimsically upon the social life of the city.

'There is abundance of good company here, and abundance of good families live here, for the sake of the good company and the cheap living; a man converses here with all the world as effectually as at London; the keeping up assemblies among the younger gentry was first set up here, a thing other writers recommend mightily as the character of a good country, and of a pleasant place; but which I look upon with a different view, and esteem it as a plan laid for the ruin of the nation's morals, and which, in time, threatens us with too much success that way.'

He notes that the city itself is spacious and 'stands upon a great deal of ground' so that the buildings are not close together or the town very populous . . . 'But as York is full of gentry and persons of distinction, so they live at large, and have houses proportioned to their quality'. He draws appropriate conclusions. 'Here', he writes 'is no trade indeed, except such as depends upon the confluence of the gentry'; and he assures his readers that the ladies 'make a very noble appearance here, and, if I may speak my thoughts without flattery, take the like number where you will, yet, in spite of the pretended reproach of country breeding, the ladies of the north are as handsome and as well dress'd as are to be seen either at the Court or the Ball'.

Defoe was describing a city confident enough to look down upon its neighbours for the rest of the century. For it had all the essentials for distinguished provincial life. Its houses and streets and public buildings were used by the gentry; it was a major market and focus for service trades and crafts; it held the Assizes twice a year which at first were the main reason for the influx of the gentry and professionals; above all, it had the horse races. They were begun in 1709, first on Clifton Ings, the meadow land, often flooded, lying to the immediate north of the city. But in 1730 the Knavesmire, part of the ancient Micklegate Stray used as pasture land, was drained and the races moved there; the building of the Grandstand by Carr of York in 1754 established them there for good. And with it all came the assemblies.

The Assembly Rooms were the focus of a mass of building in the Age of Elegance and the very symbol of the new sophisticated provincial society. At the top of Blake Street, in the heart of the city, only a few hundred yards from the Minster, the Assembly Rooms were intended to make York the centre of fashion and relaxed conviviality, the northern equivalent of Bath or London. Assemblies were already taking place when the idea of erecting a specialized building was adumbrated. At first they provided a winter entertainment for people of leisure; then they became more vigorously associated with race week, as attendance at race meetings became a national mania. There were weekly meetings for dancing and card games from about 1720 in the King's Manor; then the assemblies moved to Sir Arthur Ingram's old house beside the Minster. As if responding to the need for a change in architectural style between the seventeenth and eighteenth centuries, a number of individuals published a broadsheet in 1730 with proposals for building the rooms—for weekly assemblies, concerts and race-week balls. Enthusiasm was instant, directors were quickly found, money was subscribed and the Assembly Rooms opened in time for race week in 1732.

The aspirations and ambition of the promoters were reflected in their choice of architect. They went direct to Lord Burlington, Richard Boyle, the self-appointed and fastidious patron of architectural scholarship and correctness. Burlington had made the Grand Tour and brought back into England—and now into his own part of the country—the ideas and drawings of Palladio, the sixteenth century Italian architect whose four books on architecture had first been published in Italy in 1570. Burlington, who published Palladio's books in England in 1715, was more than anyone responsible for subjecting England to the architectural movement of Palladianism, which ruled as the dominant fashionable style for thirty years.

His Assembly Rooms at York are a version of Palladio's Egyptian Hall. There is nothing Egyptian about them, their style being Roman Corinthian. Furthermore, since Palladio only illustrated one end of such a hall, only one end of this one is presumably pure; the rest was improvised by Burlington. It is a brilliant piece of cosmetic work. The upper storey is made of timber and looks like stone; the columns are painted to look like marble. The building—like most important buildings—cost more than was anticipated, and, like many such, was in the end unsuccessful. The assemblies became less and less frequent after 1750; the lamps were lit only two nights a week; and until their restoration by the Corporation in 1951, the rooms were only used by various dancing masters and for a few concerts.

But that did not matter. By the time he finished the building, having made the drawings himself and sent wooden templates for the mouldings, Burlington had placed in York one of the seminal buildings in the history of architecture, perhaps the most pure, austere and uncompromising statement of Palladianism in the country. It set a standard for architecture and established York again as an outpost of culture and entertainment.

There was plenty of entertainment. In the central streets there were more than thirty coffee houses, all founded during the eighteenth century. From the early years of that century there was a newspaper, the *York Mercury*, from the middle of it a theatre (on the site of the present one); there was a bowling green off Marygate, where it still is, cockfighting in Bootham and Micklegate, a licensed brothel long established in Petergate ('disgraceful' said the historian Drake), regular fairs and shows with strange birds and animals and giants and dwarfs. There were grislier entertainments, like walking out to look at the heads of the Jacobite rebels on Micklegate Bar after the '45 (they stayed there until 1754), or to see the execution of Dick Turpin on the Knavesmire in 1739. There were killjoys in the Corporation, like those who persuaded it to ban people bathing naked beside New Walk in 1742; but for the most part it was full of life and relaxation; fun making was a thriving industry.

The city was also a minor centre of intellectual and artistic life. Its citizens included Francis Place, the painter and topographical artist who lived in the King's Manor, Joseph Halfpenny whose topographical drawings were published in 1807, the rare stained glass artist William Peckitt who came to York in 1753 and whose windows are to be seen in the cathedrals at York, Exeter and Lincoln, John Carr the successful architect who was Lord Mayor in 1770 and 1785, many minor artists and writers, lawyers and doctors, as well as the astronomer Goodricke, who lived in the city from 1782 to 1786.

Of the writers none made a more lasting contribution to York than Francis Drake, the surgeon, who retired and devoted the years 1729 to 1736 to assembling his book *Eboracum*, the foundation of all subsequent studies of York. His association with medicine is itself significant; in the eighteenth century York became a centre for medicine, for public health (the first Dispensary was founded in 1788) and mental health. For a general description of the life of the city in 1736, it is best to follow Drake.

'Our streets are kept clean, and lighted with lamps, every night in the winter season; and so regular are the inhabitants, to their hours of rest, that it is rare to meet any person, after ten or eleven at night, walking in them. We now reckon forty two gentlemen's coaches, twenty two hackney coaches, and twenty two hackney chairs, to be in full exercise in the city; and it will be no vanity in me to say, that though other cities and towns in the kingdom run far beyond us in trade, and the hurry of business, yet, there is no place, out of London, so polite and elegant to live in as the City of York.

'The native inhabitants of York are a civil sort of people; courteous enough to strangers, when they are acquainted a little, but shy enough before. The common people are very well made and proportioned; crookedness, either in men or women, is a rarity amongst them. The women are remarkably handsome; it being taken notice of by strangers that they observe more pretty faces in York than in any other place. The better sort of tradesmen live well in their houses ... there being few of them that do not sit down to as good a dinner, at their usual hour twelve a clock, as a very top merchant in London would provide for his family. Feasting to excess with one another is strongly in use in York, and indeed all over the north of England ... It is for this reason and their constantly living upon solid meat than few of the inhabitants are long lived in York; ... The common people speak English very ill; and have a strange affected pronunciation of some words, as *hoose, moose, coo,* for *house, mouse, cow* and so on ...'

The absence of manufactures noticed by Defoe in 1724 is confirmed by Drake in 1736. Instead of manufactures, he found that the chief support of the city was the 'resort to and residence of country gentlemen and families'. The trade that supported them was the everyday trade that is nowadays classified as service industry. It is true that an attempt was made in the 1730s and 40s to restore the industry of cloth making in factory premises. It did not succeed. For the most part York remained a market. It had a major cornmarket, a wool market (held for some years in St Anthony's Hall), a hay market in King's Square (known as the Haymarket) and, from the Restoration onwards, a very successful wholesale butter market in Micklegate. Up the Ouse came salt and lime and every year more coal. For the rest there was the usual variety of trade, with small merchants instead of the big merchant adventurers and a growing number of small shopkeepers. The innovations of the eighteenth century included comb making, horn making, drugs, toys, a glassworks established in 1797 to make glass vessels and phials, and several new steam flour mills. Three banks were founded in 1771 and more followed. With the setting up of the Assize Courts and the establishment of several asylums, York became a centre for law and lunacy.

And what did that imply for the shape of the city and the character of its buildings? It is best to start with the rivers and the work they supported, for there lay the basis of the changes that were taking place. Probably the single most significant urban improvement was the founding of the Waterworks. In 1682 the York Waterworks was established in the obsolete fortifications at the edge of the Ouse where the city walls slope down from St Leonards to the water's edge, at the point where formerly a chain had hung across the river. The old tower seemed ideal for the purpose. An engine was installed to raise the water. For the rest of the seventeenth and most of the eighteenth centuries it was worked by two horses. It the late part of the latter century the horses were replaced by a steam engine which, according to Hargrove in 1811, had a strength of 18 horse power and raised 18 gallons with every stroke at a rate of 18 strokes a minute.

From the Waterworks water was taken to all parts of the city through wooden pipes,

74

though the capacity was never adequate and water was available on certain days only. The steam engine facilitated another innovation. In the building beside the works, bathing rooms were opened. Several different types of bath could be taken; hot night-baths cost 3/6, hot day baths 2/-, tepid and cold baths 6d. Allowing for changes in the value of money, taking a bath was a very expensive luxury indeed.

The waterworks were a sign of the renewed, if never very busy, use of the river. It continued to flood and cause serious damage throughout the century. The focal point for activity on the Ouse was King's Staith on the east bank. The level of the bank was raised in 1774 and the quayside repaired. Facing it across the river, Queen's Staith was the focus of industrial use.

The Common Crane was positioned there. The Old Crane had been there since at least the fifteenth century; now in 1773, at roughly the same time as the staiths were repaired, a New Crane was set up, which came into constant use as a result of the extension of the Aire and Calder Navigation by the Selby Cut. From here York could be reached by the Ouse, which meant that York was, however indirectly, linked to Wakefield and Leeds. And although that link did not recapture for York the pre-eminence it occasionally hankered after, it did affect the city in at least one respect. It brought coal into the heart of York. By 1810, when Queen's Staith was rebuilt, the staith was mostly used by the coal trade and was for a time known as the Coal Staith.

The only bridge was still Ouse Bridge. In 1810, in an attempt to open up the city as well as to make the rivers navigable the bridge was rebuilt, to designs by Peter Atkinson. It was a protracted and painful process, like many in York; the construction of the bridge took ten years and the bridge was only opened in 1820. Until then crossing the city must have been extraordinarily inconvenient. Following the demolition of the old steep arch, the Ouse could only be crossed by a temporary ferry, as well as the two ferries at the position of the posterns at the end of the city walls—one at the end of North Street and the other at the end of Skeldergate, the positions where logically the two new major bridges were built in the nineteenth century.

Meantime a spate of bridge building was already taking place. The Blue Bridge (so called from the colour of the painted timber bridge first erected) was built in 1768 to provide continuity for the New Walk along the river bank; Monk Bridge across the Foss outside Monk Bar was built in 1794, the bridge across the Foss just below the castle in 1793 (rebuilt in 1836) and Foss Bridge itself replaced by a new stone one (also by Peter Atkinson) in 1812. What in short was happening at the end of the century and the beginning of the new one was a changing emphasis in the city as the river Foss was brought more into use and the land on its banks made more accessible. York was no longer a town lining one main river; it began to be a complex of streets crossing two rivers and using them as they had not been used before.

The development of the Foss is therefore indicative of the change in the city as a whole. Its first—and best known—use had always been as a sewer. Well into the nineteenth century the foul and nauseating condition of the Foss remained a problem. In the eighteenth century it had at least another use. By Drake's time in 1736 the Fishpond was no longer the extensive and impassable barrier it had been in the Middle Ages. An island had formed above Layerthorpe Bridge and a still larger one below it, with grass and trees on soggy land. Drake described it 'far from being firm land at present'. In the latter part of the century it took on another role.

The construction of the lock on the Ouse at Naburn had the effect of stimulating ship-building; the first iron boat in York was launched on the Foss in 1777. The river clearly had some potential. In 1793 the Foss Navigation Company was formed with a view to making it navigable to Stillington, north of the city. In the event it never got that far. But what did take place effectively changed the form of the river. The old Fishpond as such was drained in 1793. The lock at Castle Mills was constructed in 1794 and in the same year was formed Wormald's Cut, the bay on the bend of the river making a dock beside the new mills.

In 1795 the canal reached Strensall and in 1797 Sheriff Hutton. At that point work stopped and the project was never completed. Forty years later, the coming of the railways effectively killed the canals. In any case the Foss Navigation does not seem to have been a money spinner like the Aire and Calder.

Back on dry land, the changes in the city generally did not involve any major extensions or new streets outside the walls. The walls themselves were now decorative rather that defensive and began to be broken down or breached, especially towards the end of the century. Archways were broken through them, for instance the two arches beside Micklegate Bar by Carr in 1753, to allow traffic to enter more easily; and in the early years of the following century three of the barbicans in front of the bars were demolished. But generally the Georgian period in York was not one of major extension or new town planning, as happened in Bath, Edinburgh and London. York by the end of the eighteenth century had thrust out only slight extensions along the main roads, on the Mount—the main road to London and Leeds—and along Bootham—the road to the north—and outside Monk Bar—the road to Scarborough. These were fashionable streets and were lined with a few expensive houses in brick with sash windows.

The walled area of the city remained a place of gardens and closes. Cossin's map of 1727 indicates the amount of open space still in the intramural area, behind the houses; perhaps as much as a quarter of that area was unbuilt. In certain places there were bigger spaces landscaped and devoted to walks and gardens. They included the gardens of the former Dominican and Franciscan friaries on the south-west and south-east of the city which were only developed in the eighteenth and nineteenth centuries. Elsewhere streets were not so much laid out as rebuilt, with new walls along existing street fronts. To this there is one notable exception, more in character with twentieth century development than with that of its own time. That was the laying out of a new street between Davygate and Coney Street, made possible by the purchase by the Corporation and the demolition in 1745 of the ruinous Davy Hall. New Street was opened in 1746.

More typical was the modification and usually widening of existing streets. Looking at those streets today—and noting that many of them were to be widened again the following century—it seems surprising that Spurriergate and Pavement were widened in 1769, Goodramgate in 1771, Lop Lane (later transformed into Duncombe Place) in 1785, Castlegate Postern Lane (later transformed into Tower Street) in 1806 and Low Ousegate, leading to the bridge, in 1810.

Ann Middleton's Hospital was moved back and rebuilt in 1771 when Skeldergate was widened; it was still described by Hargrove in 1818 as 'a long, narrow and disagreeable street'. More common—again anticipating what would happen in the twentieth century— was the widening of corners to make easier crossings or more dignified open spaces. Typical examples were the widening of the area in front of the Mansion House (St Helen's Church-yard) in 1780 and the demolition of the chancel of All Saints Pavement in 1768 (another portion of that church was removed in the mid-twentieth century). With the ever increasing traffic the markets were widened as well. To the lasting shame of the city, the Market Cross in Pavement, a small square building of 1671, raised on columns, with a dome and lantern, was demolished in 1813.

Two years later in 1815 the Thursday Market Cross was also taken down. That was an even greater loss; Thursday market, according to Drake, had a very elegant centrepiece, completed in 1705, with five arches and a storey above with rusticated pilasters at the corners and a room inside which had been used as a school.

What really happened was that the streets began to take on their modern character. It is difficult to form an accurate picture of earlier streets and alleys because we take for granted many features which were in fact the invention of eighteenth century. In York for example the paving of streets and their repair began to be taken seriously by the Cor-poration in this period. At first it took place only outside Corporation property, other property owners being responsible for the cleaning of the land in front of theirs. An additional paver was appointed to join the 'city paver' in 1716 and gradually his work was extended to all parts of the street. Pavement justified its name and was paved during this period. So was Micklegate, lined with massive town houses.

Street cleaning was started, again at first by the Corporation only in front of its own buildings and then extended to all streets in 1786. Street lighting was set up in 1724 and extended in 1763. And the fixing of street names to the corners of streets was begun in 1782. It was a logical extension of the new habit of setting up names above shops, with symbols and coats of arms and crests. The Star Inn in Stonegate, which had lurked at the end of an alley opening off the street since the seventeenth century, was signposted in 1733 by the bar across Stonegate which features in many pictures of York.

The streets within the walls most markedly altered in the eighteenth century were High and Low Petergate, Blake Street and then St Leonard's Place, Lendal, Castlegate, Micklegate, St Saviourgate, Aldwark and the new New Street. Those outside were again existing roads with new houses—Bootham, Gillygate, Marygate, Monkgate, Blossom Street and its offshoots.

Especially symptomatic of the new elegance was the making of the urban feature of which the city seems to have been most proud. That was the construction of the New Walk. In 1719 the Corporation had already decided to beautify Lord Mayor's Walk, the path outside the walls on the north between Monk Bar and the northern tip of the Roman city; it was built up and planted with trees, presumably for the Lord Mayor to walk beneath with dignity. Encouraged by this experiment, the Corporation decided in 1732 to construct the New Walk, for people to promenade—as they are shown in Nathan Drake's celebrated drawing of 1756—between Fishergate at the southern tip of the walled city and the village of Fulford down the river. It was laid out at the expense of the Corporation under the direction of Mr Marsden, an apothecary who was also an amateur garden designer, and started on the tongue of land where the Foss joins the Ouse. Double rows of trees were planted. Then in 1738 the first Blue Bridge was built and the walk was extended down the river in the following year. At its southern end was a well known as Lady Well, with a well house designed in 1756 by Carr of York. The waters were said to be good for sore eyes. Whether they had any medicinal effect or not, the walk was certainly good for sore eyes and still is.

Back in the streets the most obvious change must have been the continual rebuilding of the houses. Building in brick was made compulsory by the Corporation after the fires of the siege of 1644; but brick houses were still a rarity until the middle of the eighteenth century. It was only towards the end of the period and in particular in the first twenty years of the nineteenth century that good new dwellings for working people began to be erected in certain areas such as Walmgate and Bishophill. Until then the change was mainly in the middle range of houses and the spectacular new mansions.

Many old decayed houses were demolished and new ones built. More common, as the demolition or restoration of buildings today frequently reveals, was the habit of rebuilding old house fronts or covering them with a skin of Georgian brick. This was partly fashion and increased their value. But it was also carried out in response to new regulations, especially those for fire prevention, which emanated from London after the Great Fire and began to be taken seriously in places like York in the 1760s. At that time the Corporation insisted that all new buildings and all existing buildings in the chief streets must have down pipes and gutters to remove the water from their roofs, thus unintentionally encouraging, as a result of constantly blocked gutters, the outbreaks of dry rot that characterize all buildings of the period. By the end of the century some of the principal streets were filled no longer with half timbered houses but with brick ones. The lead drain pipes combined with lamps and railings and bells and other details to give the surface character of the Georgian city. Small enclosed areas like Gray's Court, Precentor's Lane and Precentor's Court at either end of the Minster took on their present character; Petergate, the old Via Praetoria, had its façades changed and regulated.

Some of the older streets changed less. Watercolours of the early nineteenth century by Cave and Nicholson show a happily unkempt city, all very tatty and strewn with litter along the river banks and in the old streets. There are heaps of old timbers, warehouses with crazy hoists, steps and stairs down to the water's edge, horses and carts, washing and washerwomen, erratic roofs, drunken gutters lurching across bulging walls and a general air of cheerful seediness.

But that cannot have been true of the streets where the great houses were concentrated, in more capacious areas of the city, mediaeval rather than Roman and now in the very heart of things. Down such streets sedan chairs, licensed under an Act of 1763, were borne to the big rich mansions. Cossin's map of 1727 has drawings of some of the main ones in each margin. There are sixteen of them, three in Micklegate, three in Pavement, three in Lendal, two in St Saviourgate and one each in King's Staith, Castlegate, Davygate and Skeldergate.

They represented a dramatic revolution in taste and style. The older mansions were more rambling, spreadeagled affairs, like Buckingham House on the slopes above the right bank of the river in which the penniless Duke of Buckingham engaged in alchemy and died in 1688. It was known as 'The Duke's Place', the name commemorating a much loved figure. In the early eighteenth century the derelict mansion was demolished. By that time the new style was appearing. Before the end of the seventeenth century or perhaps at the turn of the seventeenth and eighteenth centuries, Cumberland House was built on King's Staith, with a handsome brick front on a stone plinth up which the flooded waters quickly rise, a door in the side on one of the old water lanes, elegant stone mouldings around the windows and a stone cornice below the eaves. From then onwards, influenced by the country houses going up outside the city, and in many cases designed by the same architects, the town houses of the wealthy followed thick and fast. The Red House was built in 1714, Dr Wintringham's house (later taken over and renamed the Judge's Lodging) in 1722, the Mansion House (a residence for the Lord Mayor, preceding its equivalent in London by several years) in 1730, Micklegate House about 1752, Fairfax House in 1762 and, facing it across the street of that name, Castlegate House about 1780, 20 St Andrewgate about the same time. Outside the city, but still in the nature of town houses, Acomb

House was built about 1750; more in the nature of a country house, the front of the Arch-bishop's palace at Bishopthorpe was rebuilt, in a Gothic style, in 1769.

The town houses of the wealthy were prominent elements of the scene in an arrogant, galloping city. They were not the only positive features. The theatre, formerly a transient affair of strolling players, was erected in 1736 (and rebuilt many times later), the Council began to meet in the mediaeval Guildhall when St William's Chapel was taken down, schools were founded including the Bar Convent about 1760 and Bootham School, built between 1797 and 1803. Almshouses were added to the nine or ten already in existence; one such was Wandesforde House in Bootham of 1739. On a much bigger scale, establishing York as a medical centre, the County Hospital was erected in 1740, and the asylum now known as Bootham Park Hospital in 1777, standing alone some way out of Bootham Bar in green fields and isolated grandeur, a Palladian building by a local architect. After serious allegations of mismanagement at the end of the century, Bootham was overtaken as a hospital for the humane treatment of mental illness by the Quaker foundation which was opened in 1796 as the 'Retreat for Persons Afflicted with Disorders of the Mind'. A work-house for '150 paupers' was opened in the parish of St Martin-cum-Gregory in 1767.

In addition to houses, schools and asylums, there was a minor spate of building in the shape of the growing number of Nonconformist churches. The most grimly expressive building of the movement was the Unitarian Chapel in St Saviourgate built in 1693. Twenty years before that, independent preachers began to be seen about the city, despite official discouragement and penalties.

The Society of Friends, rapidly dominating the economic life of the city, takes its origins from the visit of George Fox in 1651 when he addressed a congregation in the Minster and was thrown down the steps afterwards—a form of criticism which has un-fortunately lapsed in recent years. By 1674 the Quakers were able to adapt some existing buildings in Friargate and form a meeting house. In 1718 a new meeting house was built on the site where the present one—after one major rebuilding a hundred years later and extensive additions later still—stands as quietly and unobtrusively as you would expect from Friends. There were Baptists and Wesleyan Methodists (whose most spectacular demonstration was Centenary Chapel erected in 1840 at the end of St Saviourgate), primitive and other Methodists, United Methodists, Presbyterians, Moravians, Sande-manians and Roman Catholics, worshipping in a house in Little Blake Street (later removed when Duncombe Place was created and the church of St Wilfrid was erected).

Among the more sociable and reckless buildings put up in the eighteenth century was the Grandstand at the racecourse on the Knavesmire opened in 1754. Its architect was the local architect of the Bootham Asylum, John Carr. The work on the grandstand gave him a valuable connection with the gentry and the professionals from the city and outside it. It enabled him to found an astonishingly successful practice in Yorkshire, designing houses and public buildings in a rather heavy but thoroughly practical and substantial Palladian style.

Inside the city, in addition to some of the town houses mentioned above—such as Fairfax House and Castlegate House facing each other across Castlegate—he wholly transformed the site of the castle, last noticed being accidentally blown up after the Civil War.

The castle still had two gates, one across the Foss and the other across Little Foss, the ditch or moat around the motte. The south gate across the Foss was walled up in 1708 and the only entrance was then from the foot of Castlegate. It was rebuilt 'in handsome manner' in 1734. By that time a formidable prison, looking like a stern version of Castle Howard, had been erected at the end of the bailey facing the motte. That was the Debtors Prison, originally the County Prison, of 1705. Carr of York completed the scene when he added, on each side of the Prison and enclosing a long rectangle with the motte at one end, the Assize Courts in 1777 and the Women's Prison in 1780.

Like most of Carr's work they are dull but impressive buildings. They gave the castle a new role. The army moved out to the suburbs and built a new Cavalry Barracks on a twelve-acre site in Fulford in 1795. The castle thus became a prison and law courts; in the next century more buildings were added and the whole precinct was enclosed in a forbidding wall in 1825, now removed; finally the two prisons were united to form the Castle Museum. Carr himself became York's leading citizen. He was Lord Mayor twice and is reputed to have become a millionaire; if so, it was a unique experience for an architect.

By the end of the eighteenth century York had certainly recovered its old vitality and must have been as colourful and idiosyncratic as it was at the end of the Middle Ages. It has begun to reach out along the main roads. At the same time, the villages nearby had been experiencing much the same change and begun to reach back towards the city, so that ultimately villages like Fulford, Clifton and Acomb, each with good Georgian buildings and cottages, became constituent parts of the enlarged York.

The first thirty years of the nineteenth century thus witnessed the growth of York's most delightful suburbs, mostly now surrounded by later areas of housing. Especially desirable was the Mount, the site of the Roman burial ground on the road to Leeds and London, where a battery had been erected in the Civil War and which was now called Mount Pleasant. The Mount was the fashionable place for the building of villas, in brick or stucco, in the Regency manner, during the 1820s. Down the hill other villas and substantial houses, in Gothic and Greek styles, were lined up in the next decade. At the bottom they met Mount Vale, a terrace of neat narrow houses. It must all have looked very stately and complete.

If so, it was a delusion. The end of the eighteenth century and the first forty years of the nineteenth century saw a renewed outburst of building and redevelopment, as York shook itself into the new clothing of an urban settlement. Many of the facilities and entertainments necessary for a city now appeared. The cattle market, formerly in Walmgate, was moved to a new site—that of the former church of St Helen outside the walls—in 1828 and the disused Fishergate Bar in the city walls was opened up for access. The market in Pavement having become even busier, selling corn and poultry and eggs and butter and fruit, a huge opening was cut through to the Thursday Market, forming Parliament Street, opened in 1836, its ample space used for a street market until it was driven out by motor-cars in the nineteen-sixties.

Parliament Street was not the only street improvement. The previous year the crescent called St Leonard's Place was cut through the city walls inside the south-west part of the Roman legionary fortress on the site of the defunct St Leonard's Hospital. Forty feet wide, it was a terrace of late Georgian-type houses later adapted for use as Council Offices. It was the most serious breach ever made in the city's defensive walls, and if the city fathers had had their way it would have been only one of many.

In 1799 the Corporation ordered the taking down of all the city walls. Not having the legal right to do so, they were prevented by law. They could still remove bits and pieces. In 1808 Skeldergate Postern was removed. In 1810 it was resolved to take down Micklegate Bar. That was prevented by public outcry. Nevertheless the barbicans fronting all but one of the bars were removed—that at Monk Bar in 1825, Micklegate Bar in 1826 and Bootham Bar in 1831. In 1827 Castlegate Postern was demolished. An attempt to remove the whole of Bootham Bar was made in 1831 and was only prevented by a public meeting. But by that time, in 1829, the York Footpath Association had been formed, which gradually had the walls converted into a public footpath.

Over the following years, the footpath along the parapets saved the walls. One section, from Bootham Bar to Monk Bar, was opened as late as 1899, following restoration of the parapets and bastions which had generally been proceeding from 1840. Even so, the Corporation, having restored Walmgate Bar and the only remaining barbican in 1840, decided in 1855 to demolish the barbican once again. Having given in to public outcry, it then restored the barbican in 1864.

Individual buildings for commerce, education and social life crowded upon one another. The Museum was opened in the Abbey gardens in 1830, and a School for the Blind in the King's Manor in 1833. The Minster's Song School was erected in the same year, and, before that, a new Deanery in 1827 and the New Residence for the Canons Residentiary at the Minster in 1825. They were there in time to watch the Minster being partly burnt down by a religious maniac Jonathan Martin, brother of the painter, in 1829, and again—accidentally—in 1840. The Festival Concert Rooms, later the Museum Rooms, seating over 1700 people, were put up in 1823 and four great Music Festivals took place in the next twelve years. The gas works, new swimming baths at the south-west corner of the Manor Shore, the Proprietary School at Clifton, shortly to have its building taken over and used permanently by St Peter's School, were all set up in 1837.

In some streets new shop windows, like those inserted into the front of St William's College, were made in the first decades of the century. In the field of business, the York Savings Bank, which had been founded in New Street in 1811, moved to new premises at the corner of St Helen's Square in 1819, designed by the architect J. P. Pritchett, who had replaced the portico of the Assembly Rooms in order to widen the street for increasing traffic and trade. The York and County Bank and the York Union Bank took sites in Parliament Street and so did many other banks in the 1830s. The Yorkshire Insurance Company set itself up in St Helen's Square about the same time. And finally, the new cemetery was opened in Cemetery Road outside the walls on the site of St Andrew's Priory in 1837.

If 1837 was a bumper year for the opening of new buildings it also introduced the next chapter in the life of the city. All the components of the new city—a provincial centre of some elegance, of the gentry and the professions, of commerce and the crafts, of culture and entertainment, of law and medicine, architecture and the arts, and many branches of religion, were visibly established. Almost like a messenger of the new world the first steam packet slid up the river from Selby in 1816, the 'Waterloo Steam Packet', with crowds lining New Walk to watch the puffing monster steam up the river into the city. It was a portent. A few years later in 1825 another steam engine, Stephenson's Locomotion, was to make the historic journey from Stockton to Darlington, not far to the north; twenty-four miles to the south-west the Middleton Colliery Railway was already transporting coal, on huge cogs, down the hill to the barges moored along the Aire in Leeds. In 1839 the first railway was to arrive in York and drive through the walls to a terminus on the west bank of the river.

That was one agent of fundamental change. The other was more elusive and possibly at first unnoticed. In 1767, the shop that was to become Terry's, Bayldon and Berry's, was opened in St Helen's Square. In addition, some years earlier, in 1725, a grocer's shop was opened by Mary Tuke. Her nephew William Tuke, famous locally as a philanthropist and a leading member of the Quaker community, took the business over in 1752, was joined by his son in 1785 and began to manufacture cocoa and chocolate in a workshop behind his shop in Castlegate. It was a small business which in 1862 was transferred to Henry Rowntree and became the Cocoa Works. As well as the noise of steam engines, the smell of cocoa was in the air.

6. *Railway Street*

In 1843 a new street south of the river, parallel to North Street and cutting through the back lands of the mediaeval layout, was opened up between Tanner Row and Micklegate. Its purpose was to make a more efficient link between the ancient crossing of the river at Ouse Bridge and the new railway station at Tanner Row just inside the city walls. The man responsible for the development was George Hudson, known then and since as 'the railway king'; the street was named Hudson Street.

For all the brief grandeur of his popular title, Hudson was not an attractive or an estimable character. The son of a wealthy farmer and the inheritor of a substantial sum of money who nevertheless contrived to give an impression of having risen from rags to riches by his own exertions, Hudson entered local politics in York in 1832, became Lord Mayor in 1837 and on two subsequent occasions, its Member of Parliament. The basis of his power and influence was his chairmanship of a group of amalgamated railway companies. His activities did not stand up to scrutiny; after an enquiry into his financial transactions in 1849 he was dismissed from the chairmanship, lost his public offices and left the country.

His downfall was a national event. It provoked cartoons and comments in national papers. Locally his name stank. Hudson Street was renamed Railway Street. It was an unimaginative new name, but a correct one. For in ten years Hudson had made York not his kingdom but a railway city.

He was later, and probably wrongly, said to have aimed to 'mak all t'railways cum ti York'. It seems unlikely. He actually did his best to prevent any railways coming to York in which he was not the principal shareholder. It was indeed his failure to prevent the opening in 1846 of the Great Northern Railway's main line to London via Doncaster, Grantham and Peterborough (the route it still takes today) which led to his decline. His own company's route went via the Midlands. But whether or not he had the ambition with which he has been credited, he effectively became the symbol of the new system and the prototype of the great railway magnate. Acknowledging his historical influence, the City of York gave his name back to Railway Street in 1971.

It was a fitting tribute. For Hudson and the other railway magnates of his time initiated a new era in the history of the city and brought it back—as had often happened before in its history—into national as well as local significance after a period as a provincial centre of fashion and commerce. Such a stimulus was badly needed. Despite the spate of polite building in the eighteen-twenties and thirties, there were indications of a serious decline in the city's economic life. There were the famous Music Festivals, the proliferation of learned and cultural societies and the first meeting of the British Association in 1831; but underneath that spasmodic glitter lay an unsatisfactory situation. The city suffered from a lack of manufactures and a notable lack of public finance. The largest group of workers was employed in domestic service. Others were in the building trades, leather and transport. The market was flourishing but other aspects of life were not. The assemblies were less frequent, the races were losing their popularity and the theatre as usual was having difficulty in paying its way.

The arrival of the railways transformed the city as it transformed England, changing the relationships of town and country, of one town with another, of raw materials and manufacture, of technology and style. In that revolution York now became a centre not of manufacture but of communications. No longer a remote northern focus for provincial society, it was suddenly on the way somewhere. It shook its shoulders, stretched out and flexed its muscles with the conciousness of a new power.

The York and North Midland Railway Company approached the City authorities in 1838 with a proposal to buy and demolish part of the mediaeval walls for its station at Toft Green. The proposal was not approved; instead the company was authorized to make an archway 70 feet wide at the foot of the wall and go under it, so as not to disturb the promenade which had been established along its parapet walk. The engineer for the railway was George Stephenson.

The first train from York ran as far as Copmanthorpe on 6 April 1839. Just over a year later, on 11 May 1840, the first through-train reached London via the Midlands, leaving at 8 o'clock in the morning and reaching London at half past nine in the evening. In 1841 the station in Tanner Row, converted later to offices, was opened. A year later the last mail coach made the journey from London to York.

A new era had opened. The most obvious manifestations of that new era were the buildings in the middle of the city. The original station was a terminus, with a booking hall and offices along one side. At the end of the lines the Station Hotel was opened in 1853. There on 13 September 1854 Queen Victoria, the Prince Consort and five of their children took lunch on their way to Scotland and the Queen resolved never to stop in York again.

But a terminus station would not indefinitely suffice, for York was on the main London-Edinburgh line. The new station, bending dramatically as the line following the curve of the river sweeps round towards the west, was opened outside the walls in 1877. With its great roof 800 feet long and 234 feet wide including a span in the centre of 81 feet across the four through lines, it remains possibly the major architectural monument of post-Reformation York and one of the most spectacular of all nineteenth-century engineering works.

It was designed by Thomas Prosser. The light filters down through the roof and gives a ghostly illumination to the receding arches. The details are just as formidable and extravagant, the spandrels in the cast iron arches filled with the coats of arms of the three main companies that amalgamated in 1853 to form the North Eastern Railway—the York, Newcastle and Berwick Railway, the York and North Midland Railway, and the Leeds Northern Railway.

It was the focal point of a system of lines and bridges that changed the geography of the city and of the surrounding region. The railway bridge at Poppleton (on the York–Darlingburgh line) was completed in 1840, the Selby bridge in 1841 (replaced in 1888), the bridges at Skelton and Naburn (on the York–Doncaster line) in 1869 and 1871 respectively. More immediate in its effect upon the city was the Scarborough bridge built across the Ouse in 1845 at the start of the York–Scarborough line. When the new station was being built and the tracks were realigned and relevelled it became necessary in 1874 to raise the level of the bridge about four feet. A new footpath across the river was cantilevered out from the side of the bridge; it had previously been *between* the lines. From that line in 1872 (later extended in 1885) a branch was taken right around the city from the north to the east to form a large siding to the cattle market in Foss Islands. The most fruity of all the railway monuments was opened in 1878—the present Station Hotel.

The railways did still more for York. They had a lasting effect upon its pattern of employment. For many years, until 1905, York was one of the depots for engine repairs. More significant, it was the centre for the wagon and carriage works. They were beside Queen Street until the 1880s; then, as the North Eastern Railway concentrated more of its carriage building in York, new works were opened in the Holgate area in 1881. They were extended many times in the next few years and eventually covered 16 acres. By the end of the nineteenth century the railways were employing 5,500 workers, over half of whom were in the carriage works.

And the railways affected almost everything else as well. Within a short time the Ouse Navigation lost its passenger traffic. Goods however were still carried by it and still are; the end of the nineteenth century saw a busy trade along the river mainly in the milling and confectionary trades. Flat bottomed steamers carried wheat and sugar and glucose, lemons and cocoa, timber, cement and oil-cake and barley, sand and gravel, coal and flour. Some of that may have been stimulated by the new and larger lock at Naburn parallel to the old one. The river carried the materials and products of some of York's most characteristic industries.

In the 1840s the principal trades were in drugs, confectionery and comb-making. By the end of the century comb-making had virtually disappeared. The drugs business continued to flourish; in 1897 the old, established firm of Raimes and Company took over Micklegate House, the town house of the Bourchiers of Beningborough, and used it as a warehouse and factory until it was taken over and restored by the University of York in the 1960s. The York Glass Company, established at the end of the eighteenth century to make glass bottles, moved to Fishergate and a factory at the mouth of the Foss, where it still is, as the Redfearn National Glass Company.

Another important development was in metal work; Thomlinson Walker's the iron founders operated on a big scale both locally and nationally. They made the railings and gates outside the British Museum. In York, they were responsible for some original and now valuable shop fronts and façades in cast iron. They survived until 1911.

But the most significant developments took place in three areas of work—the cattle market, flour milling and confectionery. The cattle market had been moved to its new site outside the south-east promontory of the walls in 1826. For 144 years, until its banishment out of the city altogether in 1971, it was one of the most exotic and memorable of the scenes of York. It catered for thousands of cattle and after 1855 for tens of thousands of sheep. It occupied six acres of good urban land. There were markets at first weekly and latterly twice a week.

The flour mills had a respectable ancestry but were transformed by a technical innovation. The old Castle Mills erected after the Norman Conquest by the castle on the Foss, with a dam which flooded the land and formed the King's Fishpond, were at last taken down in 1856. The new mills were roller mills. The most productive and prosperous were those of Henry Leetham, opened in 1861 at the side of Wormald's Cut, the short cul-de-sac opening off the Foss canal; Leetham's later building (used since 1937 by Rowntree's) is one of the finest industrial structures in the city. That sparked off several similar ventures. Along the Ouse towards the end of Skeldergate two flour mills were erected soon after. They and the bonded warehouses of 1873 and 1874 gave the river side on Queen's Staith a distinctive industrial character which recent demolitions have just begun to destroy.

What however was soon to dominate the industry of the nineteenth century, and then the twentieth century, was confectionery. The two main firms were Terry's and Rowntree's. Terry's, growing throughout the eighteenth century, moved their manufactory from St Helen's Square in 1864, leaving only the shop. They moved to new premises in

Clementhorpe, just outside the city walls on the south. (They were to move further out along the same road towards Bishopthorpe in the twentieth century.) Rowntree's experienced the most dramatic expansion. The premises of Tuke and Casson in Coppergate were taken over in 1862 by Henry Rowntree. New factories were built in Tanner's Moat and North Street, well situated for transport both by water from the Queens Staith straight down the river or by rail from the station and sidings close to the factory. It also moved further out, this time to the north along the Haxby Road, in 1892. By then Rowntree's work was expanding very fast indeed. In 1879 they employed 100 workers; in 1894 they employed 893; by 1914 they employed no less than 4,066. The number went on growing and more than tripled in the twentieth century.

If York was not one of the cities that mushroomed during the climax of the industrial revolution, like Leeds, Bradford and Manchester, it nevertheless expanded with some speed and outstripped similar old cities like Norwich and Chester. The biggest growth in population coincided with the arrival of the railways and the immigration of considerable numbers of railway workers and Irish labourers in the 1840s. Whereas therefore the first forty years of the nineteenth century witnessed mainly a natural increase, with some immigration from the North Riding following agricultural changes, the next sixty years saw a huge growth from migration. The population, which had been about 17,000 in 1800, grew to about 28,000 in 1840 and then took off. By 1850 York had nearly 40,000 inhabitants and by the time of the Great War over 80,000. That numerical growth was partly due to the changing boundaries of the city. But they in turn were pushed out by the building, at first of new streets and then of whole areas of housing.

In the years following the arrival of the railways, the change most obvious to the occasional visitor to York must have been a renewed interest in the maximum use of land. Where William the Conqueror's Sheriff had cheerfully flooded a huge area and built defences: where the monasteries had sterilized open land for gardens and enclosures: where the grandees of the seventeenth and eighteenth centuries had preserved a landscape for themselves around their mansions and their town houses: the entrepreneurs of the railway era grasped the value of land, in small as well as large portions, and began to fill it up. It is from this period that date most of the tightly packed buildings in what were once the 'back lands' and were to become (in the felicitous phrase of a twentieth-century planner) the 'shack lands' of York. The gardens lying behind the mediaeval Georgian street façades became courts and alleys and yards for workshops and small businesses; the gardens of the mansions were hemmed in and the mansions themselves gutted and squashed into new shapes to accommodate trades and industries. The back of town houses received additional wings or merely had wings thrust upon them from neighbouring properties. In short, most of the problems besetting a modern planner concerned with conservation and the restoration of historic buildings were then created. They were not problems for the Victorian developer or for the city's authorities; they could cheerfully watch the city filling up and increasing in density at the centre—a classic case of the 'implosion' of Victorian cities.

The most important—and in many ways the most successful—of such attempts to use land fully and create more space was the transformation of Foss Islands, the area discussed in the last chapter in relation to the Foss Navigation. In the 1840s Foss Islands was described as a 'stinking morass'. The description was deserved. When the old fishery had been maintained—at first under royal control, later in private hands—the Fishpool had been a reasonably attractive stretch of water. Over the years the water had receded, as eighteenth-century maps reveal, leaving not just the two main islands but a large area of waterlogged land. It was clearly worth draining it and putting it to some use.

In 1850 the Corporation adopted the Public Health Act of 1848, taking over the powers previously exercised by the City Commissioners, a shadowy and ineffectual body which seems, in the words of an historian, to have done little in the early nineteenth century beyond constructing 'defective sewers of inadequate length'. In its new enthusiasm for sanitation and improvement, the Corporation took over the Foss Navigation and agreed to drain Foss Islands. There was ample evidence from the cholera and typhus epidemics of 1832 and 1847 of the dangerous state of the stagnant river and the waterlogged land. It was drained in 1855. The Castle Mills were taken down, the bridge was widened, the Navigation was formally closed in 1859, and the Foss, with a new lock (reconstructed in 1889) became once again a useful small river giving access to places upstream and now to the mills on Wormalds Cut. In addition the city had a large new area of reclaimed land. It was soon put to use for the goods station. Across it, furthermore, was constructed a new street, Foss Islands Road, built on the made-up land between 1854 and 1856, in place of the devious and untrustworthy footway that had previously existed.

The significance of that road cannot be overstated. It meant that a significant portion of the route encircling the city walls was at last in existence. The rest of that circuit depended upon other works and bridges which were rapidly being constructed. The opening of the railway provoked requests for a better road system near the station and in particular for a new bridge across the Ouse nearer to the station than Ouse Bridge and giving access to the oldest part of the city across the river, to the north and to the east. As new road approaches were planned and made, proposals to erect such a bridge were put in 1838, 1847 and 1857, and the bridge was finally erected in 1860. Or not quite. Designed by an engineer with the ominous name of Dredge, the new bridge fell into the river in 1861, killing five people; the bits recovered were sold to Scarborough and incorporated into the Valley Bridge. Meantime another engineer, Thomas Page, was commissioned to produce a new design. Lendal Bridge was opened in 1863.

It was for thirty-one years a toll bridge and paid for itself comfortably. For its time it was thus clearly in the right place, which was the position of the old ferry, crossing the

Ouse from landings at the ends of the city walls where they stopped on the banks of the river and where, in the Middle Ages, a chain had been slung across for defence. The old ferryman was the beneficiary of a public subscription, which sent him away with a horse and cart and a sum of cash.

With the erection of the new station outside the walls in 1877, its approaches had to cut through the walls. In that year two arches were made in them. The roads twisting through them provided a continuous route and also gave access to the porte-cochère of the new station. They were roughly on the line of the old Thief Lane which had run from Micklegate Bar to North Street postern. And the new roads involved some ingenious engineering work. At one side in 1876 Queen Street was slung across the lines leading to the old station; on the other a new roadway, Leeman Road, was driven back under the lines through a wide dark tunnel dubbed ironically—and permanently—Marble Arch.

Downstream, at the other end of the city's defensive wall, a second new bridge was erected in 1881, this time on the line of the old 'Castlegate Ferry' which had plied between Skeldergate Postern and the Castle. Skeldergate Bridge made the circuit almost complete. Castle Mills Bridge, crossing the Foss immediately after Skeldergate Bridge crosses the Ouse, and Layerthorpe Bridge, crossing the Foss again at the end of the wall near Monk Bar, provided the necessary continuity for a ring road round the walls. The only break in the geometric neatness of this arrangement was the position of Lendal Bridge just inside the line of the wall and the consequent breaches through the wall at Station Avenue.

The encircling road did more than provide a way round the walls and some badly needed additional land; it effectively transformed the basic configuration of the city in a way that characterizes nearly all Victorian development. York was now potentially no longer a small walled settlement, with a few radial roads leading out from the old gates in the direction of other major towns. The opening up of the land all round the walls, not just along the radial routes, meant that a new three-dimensional, spatial entity was brought into being. The land around the old city in irregular concentric rings could in time be developed; the bulk of new building could take place there. The building type which occupies most urban space, housing, could find sufficient sites either just outside the walls, or, with roads joining through them, just inside. The result was that the old walled city became within fifty years no longer the whole city, but an unusually defined central area for the specialized functions of a modern city.

What changes took place in that central area? The most ruthless were the widenings and realignments of existing streets to accommodate an increased number of movements and the commercial functions of the city centre. A good example is the road leading towards the Minster from Lendal ferry, where now was Lendal Bridge. It had changed its name many times, and was known in the early nineteenth century as Back Lendal. Following the erection of the Yorkshire Museum in 1830, it became Museum Street. Now, in

1846, it was widened. At its upper end it became Lop Lane, which in the nineteenth century became Little Blake Street and then between 1859 and 1862 Duncombe Place, the present wide road leading to the west front of the Minster.*

Named after Dean Duncombe, who promoted the plan and contributed to the cost of the work, Duncombe Place was partly rebuilt on one side and laid open, with a landscaped garden, on the other. In its state of completion at the end of the century, it must have been a well-used and coherent open space, a condition noticeably spoiled when in 1903 the road was continued along the south side of the Minster in the form of Deansgate. Duncombe Place was now part of the main road to Scarborough, where formerly it had been a handsome city centre avenue.

Other street widenings took place increasingly towards the end of the century—in the eighties, the Micklegate end of Skeldergate, the corner of Gillygate and much of Holgate Road; in the nineties, Barker Hill (renamed to its inhabitants' disgust St Maurice's Road when the new church was erected), Lord Mayor's Walk (preserving the trees planted there in the last chapter), Coppergate, Goodramgate, parts of Davygate and Nessgate in the heart of the city; in the early years of the twentieth century, Piccadilly (effectively a new street) and Pavement. The effect of these widenings can be seen in the number of late nineteenth century façades in the city centre, which often give a false impression of the age of the buildings; in many cases they are merely refacings to much older houses which still lurk behind the brick façades and hug their history to themselves.

Such improvement was typical of the few other changes made inside the walls. At the eastern end of the Minster, the Bedern, the old courtyard of the College of Vicars Choral of the Minster, which had degenerated and become by the 1840s a warren of infested houses, was cleared and the court converted into a thoroughfare, since when it has declined steadily again, not this time into a residential slum but an industrial backwater.

More successful was the redevelopment of the notorious Water Lanes. There were three of these lanes, crossing from Castlegate down the slopes to the banks of the Ouse at Kings Staith. The first—starting at the Ouse Bridge end—had become Carr Lane, the second Thrush Lane and the third, on the edge of the site of the former Franciscan friary, Friargate.

In 1818 Hargrove described the lanes as containing the 'poorest and the most disorderly part of the population'. When improvements were made to the Kings Staith in 1851, the first Water Lane was demolished and rebuilt as King Street. In 1876 proposals were made for rebuilding the remaining Water Lanes as part of the opening up of that section of the city with a new road from Nessgate to Tower Street immediately to the

---

* A quaint series of names was taken by the lane that leads from St Sampson's Square to Swinegate—Ficteles Lane, Footless Lane, Finkle Street and Mucky-Pegg Lane.

south of Clifford's Tower. Like almost every other proposal put to the Corporation in the nineteenth century it was modified, rejected, resurrected, modified and rejected again; having presumably run out of breath, the Corporation finally decided to get on with the work and created Clifford Street in 1881. In doing so, the Corporation adopted a policy that was to recur in many towns in the nineteenth and twentieth centuries—the combination of slum clearance and road building at the same time. The making of new roads and the clearing of unfit housing have ever since gone hand in hand.

On the other side of the river, still inside the walls, a major development was the laying out of Priory Street in 1854 and the formation of a substantial area of workers' housing in the streets between it and the city walls in Bishophill. It was the land of the former Holy Trinity Priory, undeveloped since the Reformation except for the Duke of Buckingham's house, which had itself been demolished following his lapse into poverty at the end of the seventeenth century. For a long time unrecognized for what it was, that area is now in considerable demand; for it is good quality, low-cost housing, mostly built in the twenty years between 1851 and 1871, and extended down to the coal staith in the next few years.

The other area inside the walls developed densely in the years following the arrival of the railways was Walmgate, within the eccentric bulge in the old city on the left bank of the Foss, partly flooded by the Fishpool and enclosed by its own city wall later than the rest of the mediaeval city. That elbow of land was always underprivileged, though it contained two mediaeval churches—of St Denys and St Margaret. Walmgate was its spine, leading from Fossgate and Foss Bridge to Walmgate Bar and the road to Hull.

Most of the new development in that area revolved about George Street, which runs southwards from Walmgate to Fishergate Bar in the walls and to Fishergate. George Street has a history of change as symptomatic as that of Duncombe Place. In the mediaeval period part of it was Nowtgate (a road for cattle), and the other part, from the bend in the middle to the city wall, was part of Fishergate—Fishergate Within. With the removal of the cattle market to its new site just outside the walls, Nowtgate was a cattle route going in the opposite direction. At the end of it, Fishergate Bar, which had been blocked for three and a half centuries, was opened up to the cattle market in 1827. That part of the street—now George Street—was rebuilt at the same time; the Walmgate end was rebuilt and widened in 1844. Into the houses around George Street flocked most of the Irish immigrants in the 1840s; one of the streets was named Rosary Street and the Catholic church of St George, designed by the eminent architect, J. A. Hansom, was erected in 1850, its style as well as its name giving continuity to the religious life of the district. Of its poverty more is said later in this chapter.

Outside the walls, in closer contact with the streets within since the making of new arches beside the old bars in the 1860s, building went on remorselessly. The windmills, which had surrounded the city in picturesque idiosyncracy for several hundred years, were one by one taken down. (Only one survives—the late eighteenth-century mill on Holgate Hill, its sails taken down only in 1930.) In place of the mills spread street after street of houses.

The most hectic period of house building was between 1830 and 1860. In the fifties at least 200 houses a year were being erected; and although that rate was not kept up, the character of the city owes much to the rapid building of houses in that period, almost all in a dark greyish brick, with slate roofs, the minimum of decorative features, some austere neo-Georgian woodwork around the front door and small patches of grass in the more prosperous streets.

While the larger houses indulged in a certain amount of unassertive display, the lower-cost houses were all remarkably alike—the direct result of the adoption by the City of the 1848 Public Health Act in 1850 and the passing of bye-laws requiring minimum room sizes, ventilation and access. The first bye-laws in York came into effect in 1859.

Although the building up of the suburbs did not follow a methodical plan, it is possible to draw a general picture of the pattern of growth. In the first thirty years of the nineteenth century, discussed at the end of the last chapter, development was scattered inside the walls and just outside them, with the addition of some substantial and elegant villa building of a Regency type mainly along the road south-west to London. That included the stuccoed houses of the Mount, what was once Mount Pleasant, Mount Vale and the open fields around, and such hidden gems as Mount Parade, behind and at right angles to the main road.

The next phase, in the thirties, included the two major intramural streets—Parliament Street and St Leonard's Place—and the modifications to the streets between them, making an improved opening through the heart of the commercial centre. At the same time began what was to be a continuous development for the rest of the century—the building up of the Groves area outside the walls to the north-east, in depth on both sides of the main road to Malton and Scarborough, a huge area of land between the Foss and Wiggington Road, north of the tree-lined Lord Mayor's Walk.

In addition to the development of the Groves, the forties saw the housing of Irish immigrants in Walmgate and of the railway workers around Railway Street and outside the walls to the west of the railway lines, as well as more substantial houses and shops in the Mount, smaller streets opening off Blossom Street, and terraced housing in Gillygate outside Bootham Bar.

The fifties and sixties saw the making of the Bishophill area inside the walls, new streets off Nunnery Lane joined to that area through Victoria Bar (which had been cut through the wall in 1840), and five major developments outside the walls—Clementhorpe to the south, the barracks area near the old Cavalry and the new Infantry Barracks on

93

Fulford Road, the streets south of Lawrence Street (Hull Road), Layerthorpe east of the Foss, and the clumsily respectable area around St Paul's Square and the Holgate Road.

In the eighties, the area known as the Foundry district near the railway goods yard, reached through Marble Arch, was built up with workers' houses when the Phoenix Foundry moved there from Piccadilly. And in the nineties some more prosperous housing was erected—on the Marygate estate, in Bootham and Clifton and Heworth, along the Scarcroft and Wiggington Roads.

These were essentially suburban extensions for the expanding middle classes. Some of the areas already contained eighteenth- or late eighteenth-century houses and had begun to fill up in the sixties and seventies; others grew out from new roads, such as Scarcroft Road, built to provide a link between two of the old radial roads; others were related to new facilities, such as the hospitals on the north-east and the cemetery on the south-east; others again were generated by the radial roads themselves, such as the Hull Road and the nearby, new Heslington Road. If the 1830s had seen a formidable amount of public building, the last decade of the nineteenth century saw the century out in almost a fever of house building. In the last year of that century nearly five hundred houses were either completed or under construction, on all sides—north towards Haxby and Huntingdon, south towards Fulford, west towards Acomb, east along the Hull Road. And still the spaces between existing buildings were filling up.

The overall effect of this mass of building was to establish more firmly than before, and on a more clearly defined geographical basis, the social stratification of the city. In all the main periods of nineteenth-century building, the contrast between desirable and less desirable areas became more marked. Whereas the urban developments of the eighteenth century had placed rich and poor houses together in the same areas, differentiated by their access rather than their orientation, the nineteenth century put distance between them and set like with like. Especially the second half of the century. In those fifty years, the prosperous gathered at the Mount, Heworth, Clifton and Fulford; the less prosperous at Nunthorpe, Cemetery Road, Holgate Road, Layerthorpe and near the workhouse to the north; the nearly destitute in the old city.

That meant that by the end of the century there were at least three social groups, whose precincts indentified them sufficiently clearly. There were the old town houses converted into slums for the very poor, together with areas of inadequate housing, some (now demolished) in rows of back-to-backs, though never on the scale of Leeds and the West Riding; there were the new districts of working class terrace housing, like those by Holgate Road, for the prosperous artisans; and a little further out there were the houses of the servant-keeping classes, on the Mount and at Dringhouses or Clifton (to which the Rowntree family moved at the turn of the century). At its upper end, it was still however a middle class society. The gentry and the truly fashionable had moved out altogether.

As the city grew, its boundaries were extended. In 1884 the York Extension and Improvement Act incorporated into the city several formerly independent townships, not without much protest and foreboding on the part of those about to be incorporated, remarkably similar to the anxieties expressed in the early nineteen-seventies about local government changes and reorganization. Those townships included Holgate, Dring-houses, Knavesmire, Fulford and Clifton. The boundaries were extended again in 1893, and after that more widely in 1937—when the land surrounding Dringhouses, Middle-thorpe and Acomb, where most of the twentieth-century development had taken place, was brought in as well.

While the city's housing expanded and surrounded the old city throughout the nine-teenth century, back in the middle the fever for rebuilding was nearly as great. There it was concentrated upon public buildings. It brought in eminent architects with a national reputation or made the reputations of local ones. John Carr and his partner Peter Atkinson had dominated the architectural scene in the eighteenth and early nineteenth centuries; J. P. Pritchett and G. T. Andrews dominated it up to the eighteen forties; a great variety of architects thereafter. The architects who shaped York in the nineteenth century in-cluded William Wilkins (the Yorkshire Museum), Ridsdale Tate (the Tempest Anderson Hall), John Harper (St Peter's School, St John's College), J. P. Pritchett (the Yorkshire Savings Bank, the portico to the Assembly Rooms), G. T. Andrews (St Leonard's Place, Priory Street, the old Railway Station, the Yorkshire Insurance Company), George Goldie (St Wilfrid's R.C. Church), George Fowler Jones (Heworth and Clifton churches and the entry to Museum Gardens), W. G. Penty (Leetham's Mill, the Burton Stone public house), George Walton (the interior of Elm Bank Hotel) and W. H. Brierley (Scarcroft, Haxby Road and Poppleton Road schools).

Between them they punctuated the city with a variety of buildings, public and private, in a bewildering mixture of styles and varying degrees of sophistication, in brick and stone and tile and slate, favouring if anything a kind of gutless neo-Gothic style but by no means exclusively. Andrews' Yorkshire Insurance Company head offices in St Helen's Square had established a calm Renaissance manner for such palaces of commerce and finance (appropriately it was a version of the Farnese Palace); on the other hand hotels like the Dean Court favoured a late Gothic manner. The Museum of 1830 was Grecian; a more astonishing version of Grecian was added to it in the form of the Tempest Anderson Hall of 1912, which was built wholly—pilasters, capitals, metopes, triglyphs, everything—of *in-situ* concrete, one of the most staggering feats of reinforced concrete design. The Theatre Royal was rebuilt several times until by 1880 it looked suitably Gothic and ecclesiastical for a site so near the Minster—salvation and damnation rejoicing in the same style. When the façade was rebuilt in 1880, the elegant stone arched arcade across the front, built in 1832 to match the elegant façades of the new houses on the opposite side of the crescent, was re-erected as a garden wall or screen to a property in Fulford Road where it still stands, badly decayed and partly derelict.

Schools were just as varied. The Wilberforce School for the Blind was established in the King's Manor in 1835 and new wings were added to it at the end of the century, including a house for the superintendent in a deceptively authentic-looking Tudor style. A unique contribution to architectural history were the three schools designed at the end of the century by W. H. Brierley, at Scarcroft, Haxby Road and Poppleton Road, an ingenious interpretation of official school requirements and functional demands in a modified Art Nouveau style. Medical buildings were more classical, the most distinguished being the County Hospital in Monkgate, a replacement of the eighteenth century building in 1851, and the most idiosyncratic the York Dispensary in Duncombe Place by Edmund Kirby of 1899, built in apparently imperishable moulded bricks. The same architect was also responsible for the most exotic of the banks, Barclays of 1901, equally red, smooth and shiny.

In a different sphere the military extended their property and their operations. The Cavalry Barracks had been built on a conveniently flat and open site between the Fulford Road and Walmgate Stray in the eighteenth century. The Infantry Barracks was set up beside it in 1874 and two years later, outside the city, Strensall Common was given to the military as well. For such activity a suitable house had to be made available for the General Officer Commanding, and that was the building known as 'Government House' in Bootham on the corner of Grosvenor Terrace, one of the new substantial suburban streets created in the second half of the century. To complete the military provision, York Castle ceased to be a civil prison and was used solely for military detention.

As in most other towns, the Victorian period was the heyday for the battle of the styles waged over church buildings. In York new churches were not really necessary in the intramural area, where indeed there was a superfluity of churches already, except for the needs of a growing number of Nonconformists and Roman Catholics. Methodism and Quakerism flourished, the former rejoicing in some splendid meeting houses, the latter concentrating not so much on the suitably reticent Meeting House whose entrance was now in Clifford Street but on educational enterprises, especially the schools at Bootham and the Mount. The Presbyterians built a dignified church in Priory Street in 1879; the Catholics built St George's in 1850 and the hideous church of St Wilfrid close to the Minster in 1864. New buildings were put up to accommodate the Poor Clares who settled in Lawrence Street in 1872 and the Sisters of Charity of St Paul the Apostle who built a convent and school in Monkgate between 1870 and 1875.

The Established Church built mainly in the suburbs—sound Gothic edifices such as the churches at Heworth and Clifton, both made necessary by suburban developments. Otherwise the period is marked by two significant changes. The mediaeval church of St

Crux in Pavement was declared unsafe and was demolished, to the general regret, in 1888. And the old College of St William, east of the Minster, which had lost its ecclesiastical role after the Reformation, been used by Charles I for his printing presses just before the Civil War, as a town house and then as tenements, was bought in 1900 by Francis Green, who was engaged in restoring the Treasurer's House, and sold by him to the York Diocesan Trustees for use by Convocation.

Inevitably, as in every other town or city that experienced unprecedented expansion in the course of the Industrial Revolution, York had a seamier side. It was not so much the direct result of rapid expansion as a reflection of the fact that the Industrial Revolution had to some extent passed York by and left it without the resources to make progress in civic improvements. The desultoriness of the city in tackling the problems was as much due to lack of money as to the apparently immutable indecisiveness of the civic authorities and perhaps a certain native complacency. To anyone looking closely at York the problem of poverty must have been aggressively obvious; but it seems to have needed Seebohm Rowntree's classic study of *Poverty* in 1901 to bring home by means of statistics to the authorities that, far from being happier than places like London, it had in fact a worse record of poverty. The areas inhabited by the poorest people were those characterized by the same phenomena as every other depressed area of the time—low levels of income, high densities, poor living conditions and recurring problems of water supply and drainage.

Whereas there had been some immigration in the 1820s and 1830s mainly from the North Riding, the great period of immigration was the 1840s, with people crowding in from the West Riding and from Ireland after the famines. The Irish constituted the core of the immigration problem in the nineteenth century. In 1841 there were 327 Irish in York; in 1851 there were 1,928. They were concentrated in certain areas, usually keeping in defined groups by their place of origin—Mayo or Sligo for example. These were the Bedern and the area around St Margaret's Church and the new St George's in the Walmgate district. The serious outbreak of typhus that scourged the city in 1847 was associated with that district, and even towards the end of the century the infant mortality rate was exceptionally high. In the 1880s one child in three in the Walmgate area died before the age of one.

Other parts of the city were affected by bad housing too. Characteristically the poor crowded into the older areas. At the bottom of Skeldergate, where a serious outbreak of cholera occurred in 1832, was a court with the sinister nickname of 'Hagworm Nest'. In the middle the poor crowded, not as in the West Riding and Lancashire into cellars, but into the old decayed town houses of the wealthy families who had now, with the help of the railways, found it more satisfactory to have their town houses in London. Huge Georgian mansions like Peaseholme House, Bishophill House, Micklegate House and Fairfax House were stripped and became warehouses or workshops or warrens of rented rooms. The poor were thus to be found in districts such as Peaseholme Green, the Water Lanes (until the 1880s), Fossgate and Walmgate. In such areas Rowntree considered that 70 per cent were living in conditions of primary poverty at the end of the nineteenth century.

The core of the problem tackled by the medical officers of health under the Public Health Act of 1872 (the first was appointed a year later) was water supply and sanitation. In the very area of the city in which the poor were most densely congregated the disreputable river Foss still wound its sluggish way down to the dam and spread around any germs that it picked up on its festering banks. (The notorious state of the river did not prevent the city from building public baths, a hospital and a fever hospital beside it.) Eight thousand midden privies still flavoured the courts and streets by the end of the 1880s. They were much used; in the 1850s there were in many areas between four and fourteen families per privy. Things were not much better where sewers existed; in flood conditions it was not unknown for the sewers to work in reverse and fill the cellars.

The improvement of the sewage system begun soon after the adoption of the Public Health Act took a long time to reach most parts of the city. Meantime the water supply was steadily improved. The old waterworks at St Leonard's Tower having become quite inadequate for the city on its new scale, a new waterworks was built from 1846 to 1849 with filter beds at the Acomb Landing and a big reservoir on Severus Hill above Acomb. Following that, baths were increasingly installed in houses. In 1850 only 20 houses supplied by the waterworks had a bath; by 1900 about 10 per cent of the houses supplied by it had one. And by that time 40 per cent of the houses had a watercloset.

The improvements in water supply and drainage were a signpost to the increasing power and responsibility of local government. In 1832 York had become a Parliamentary borough and in 1836 it became a municipality, with boundaries the same as those of the ancient liberty of the city. Following the Municipal Reform Act, the Public Health Acts of 1848 and 1872 and the Housing Act of 1890 the Corporation took its duties increasingly seriously. It was in effect towards the end of the century that the results of legislation and reorganization began to be seen; the period from 1850 to 1900 can be considered as that of the consolidation and maturing of local government in York and the extension of its responsibilities and influence.

The first tram ran in 1880, from Fulford to Castle Mills Bridge; for a short experimental period there were steam trams and then horse trams; then the rails were extended to Clifford Street, across the river and up to the Mount in 1882 to a terminus at the corner of Dalton Terrace. The General Post Office in Lendal was opened in 1884. A few years previously, the first telephone was installed in 1878 and a year later was opened the new permanent building for the York Exhibition on a site then known as Bearpark's Garden; the building became the City Art Gallery in 1891. In that year new Council

Offices and a new Council Chamber were opened adjoining the Guildhall: the next year the Public Library, first mooted thirty years before and the subject of endless disagreement, and at the same time the new Fire Brigade headquarters, Law Courts and Police Station in Clifford Street, also the subject of constant dispute.

General civic improvements followed. At the end of the century an Electricity Generating Station was set up in Foss Islands (the Gas Company was already there in Layerthorpe), whose most notable modern features are the Cooling Tower built after the Second World War and the footbridge across the Foss erected in 1951. The city was first lit by electricity in 1899. Other improvements included the laying out of Terry Avenue along the bank of the Ouse opposite the New Walk. The bank was piled and stabilized and planted with trees in 1893. The city was once again elegant as well as bustling, its streets and avenues swarming with people walking, with horses and carts and wagons. But also with something revolutionary. The great bicycle boom in England was in 1896 and 1897. For that machine the flat land of the plain of York and the streets of the city with only the gentlest of hills were ideally suited. From the eighteen-nineties to the present day tens of thousands of bicycles have passed along the streets of York daily, and provided one of the most characteristic features of the place.

Two very different events at the end of the period can be taken as indicating some of the fundamental influences at work in the late Victorian city. The first was the fate of the old George Inn in Coney Street. Erected at the beginning of the seventeenth century, it was a magnificent complex of sprawling buildings, with a huge courtyard, between Coney Street and the banks of the river. In 1855 it was offered for sale, the advertisement being addressed 'To Capitalists and Builders'. It was eventually sold and demolished in 1869. It stood on the site of the present store of Leak and Thorp. It was, as the advertisement clearly spelled out, a symptom of what was to characterize the city centre (like all city centres) increasingly with the passing years—the profitability of removing old and wasteful buildings and replacing them with shops and offices, a trend that is still with us today.

The second event was just as definitive and much more positive. In 1901 Joseph Rowntree, having moved his factory out to the Haxby Road and his family to Clifton, set up the Joseph Rowntree Village Trust and, inspired by the ideas of Ebenezer Howard (whose book *Tomorrow: a Peaceful Path to Real Reform* was published in 1898 and shortly afterwards reissued as *Garden Cities of Tomorrow*), started to build the first garden village— at New Earswick, a few miles to the north of the Cocoa Works. It was not just a housing scheme for employees of the Cocoa Works; indeed it was laid down that no more than one-third of the residents should be employed there.

The creation of New Earswick was a seminal event, of lasting importance not so much to York as to the whole country. It established the viability of new town building to significantly improved standards; it experimented with many of the features that have since become commonplace in urban and rural development—the cul-de-sacs, the cottage-type houses with through living rooms, sunny aspect and generous gardens, the provision of community facilities, the Folk Hall, the primary school related to the housing areas, the ample trees and thick planting. The village was planned and the buildings designed by Raymond Unwin and Barry Parker, had originally 500 homes and was separated from the city (and from the cocoa works) by a green belt. It blazed a trail for Letchworth, Welwyn Garden City and ultimately the New Towns and was possibly York's most lasting legacy from the Victorian age.

But this chapter must end in the centre of the city, in the colour and life of the second half of the nineteenth century. It may have been a bad time for the poor and the under-privileged; for the better off and the propertied it must have been as vital, as noisy and boisterous as at any time in its history. In streets hurriedly being filled up and rebuilt, amid the crashes of falling masonry and the clouds of dust, against a background of the noise of trains and trams, under the gathering smoke from innumerable domestic fires, surrounded by a growing number of banks and shops and offices and hotels, life for some people must have been full, rewarding and amusing. The bicycles rattled along the streets, the pleasure steamers plied up and down the Ouse, in what seems now to have been a series of long hot summers, and moored at the landing just below Lendal Bridge.

Above that landing the gentlemen of the Yorkshire Club took their luncheon and slept in leather chairs below walls lined with portraits of famous horses, or dined formally in the evening and looked out across the river from the Dining Room or the Smoke Room. On the other side of Lendal Bridge the horses on which they had ridden from the country, or which had pulled their carriages, could rest in Botterill's Horse Repository, an exotic red and yellow Byzantine building with ramps inside, up which the horses were led to their stalls—a kind of multi-storey horse park. The Yorkshire Club still functions, though much reduced in size. But when the upper floors of the Horse Repository were demolished in 1965 it seemed the end of an era—an era which had begun with Railway Street and taken shape and form with the erection of Lendal Bridge and the Yorkshire Club beside it in 1868.

RIVER FOSS

7. The Precinct

Before the turn of the century, the first motor car was seen in the streets of York. After the First World War, the number of cars steadily increased. In the years following the Second World War they became effectively an invasion. If the use of the river was the making of ancient, mediaeval and Georgian York and the arrival of the railway was the generator of Victorian York, the coming of the motor car was a decisive influence upon the planning and architecture of the modern city, affecting its functions and its environment and dominating the controversies about York's present and future. The motor car will thus serve to introduce the story of York in the twentieth century.

At the beginning of the century, the tramcars were still battling their way through the streets of the city. In 1909 the Corporation bought the trams from the York Tramways Company and in the same year electrified them. Even so, the trams presented constant problems, especially where they had to make their way over old bridges or past the defensive walls or through the gates and bars. In 1915 therefore petrol buses were added to the trams and in 1935 the trams were discarded altogether.

That the Corporation was involved in these developments was symptomatic of the vastly increased responsibilities and expanded role of local government in the early years of the twentieth century. In York, as in all cities and towns, local government was no longer—as it had been described in the nineteenth century—concerned mainly with drains and policemen; it was engaged in an ever widening group of activities, affecting almost every aspect of the life of the community. In 1902 it took over responsibility for education. In 1930 it accepted responsibility for the poor. And increasingly it engaged in trading activities. By the middle of the twentieth century it was one of the principal employers of labour in the city. The electricity undertakings had been begun in 1900 and increased with every year. The use of libraries expanded. The new library was built in 1927 within the corner of the Roman wall, near the Multangular Tower.

The Precinct

But the main—and visually the most effectual—part of its work was housing. Under the 1890 Housing of the Working Classes Act little had effectively been done, even though in the second half of the nineteenth century, Dr Laycock had reported to the Commissioners of Property about the state of property in the Bedern: 'Of 98 families living there, 67 have only one room for all persons, 18, two rooms, 13 three rooms or more'. Under that Act only nineteen houses were condemned. More effective was the 1909 Housing, Town Planning etc. Act. Under that, slum clearance began seriously for the first time. It was estimated at the time that there were 1,519 back-to-back houses, all of which required attention. It was also pointed out that the new housing being erected at the time was inferior.

It was effectively with the 1919 Act, which made government subsidies available for council housing and was therefore the origin of 'council housing', that the Corporation began to act on a substantial scale. By that time it was estimated that the city had a shortage of about 560 houses; it also needed to demolish about 450 houses in the area around Walmgate. Adding those together, and adding to it also a number of other requirements, it seemed that the city needed 1,250 new houses straight away.

In 1915 the Corporation had purchased the Tang Hall estate immediately to the east of the built-up area. It now began to build there, settling many of the people moved from Walmgate as well as others. It was a major development, some 288 acres in extent, and it contains the earliest council houses in York. At the same time a start was made on the estate at Acomb which was, over the years, to become the major expansion area for York. Here, however, sites were sold for development by private builders, as well as being used by the Corporation itself.

Other areas of land were bought in Heworth and in Holgate and in Burton Stone Lane in the late 1920s. Clearance of substandard housing began to speed up. More houses were demolished in Walmgate and houses in the Layerthorpe, Navigation Road and Hungate areas began to be cleared. Between 1919 and 1939 nearly 2,000 houses were demolished and nearly 7,000 people had to be rehoused. To accommodate them nearly 5,000 council houses were built. As a result only about 500 seriously inadequate slum houses, with another possible 3,000 requiring treatment, remained by the beginning of the Second World War. The slum houses were cleared in the years immediately following it.

The second main area of activity undertaken by the Corporation was the implementation of the Town Planning Act of 1925. Under that Act local authorities were required to carry out town planning studies for towns with populations of more than 20,000, and to prepare schemes in anticipation of future developments. There was an emphasis on roads. The authority in York divided the city theoretically into eight areas and applied planning policies to each. More important, it made plans to encircle the whole city with a ring road, crossing the Ouse at Clifton and eventually linking to all the major radial routes. The first part of it was constructed from 1929 onwards. That was Kingsway, curving round the city on its north-west edge. The road was conceived as a dual carriageway with houses on each side and a large space of grass in the middle. The Corporation later changed its mind and allowed the erection of houses and other buildings across the line of the road. The grand by-pass road thus emerged as some unkempt, derelict land, partially littered with broken-down vehicles, and occupying an oddly incomprehensible wedge in a corner of the city. In the middle of the city it was proposed to build a road from Pavement to Peaseholme Green and widen Layerthorpe so as to relieve the Scarborough Road. That road, from Pavement to Peaseholme Green, was ultimately built after the Second World War.

The physical changes in the city reflected a steady development in its economic life and an increasing specialization in its work. In 1911 the confectionery industry in York employed 3,737 people, which was less than the number employed by the railways. The inter-war period saw the expansion of the confectionery industry, mainly because of the expansion of Rowntree and Company. By the Second World War it dominated the employment pattern of the city, employing 12,274 people. That represented 30 per cent of York's insured working population. The railways employed 13 per cent. An important difference, however, between employment by the railways and employment by the confectionery industry was that in the latter more than half the employees were women and girls.

Other developments occurred at the same period. The British Sugar Corporation built its factory at Acomb in 1927 but employed small numbers. The printing industry increased its work; over 1,000 employees worked in the printing industry by 1939. There was a significant increase in the service industries and in the distributive trades, in government services both national and local. The Market changed, but not fundamentally; the number of sheep sold decreased, the number of cattle and pigs increased. In company with the whole country York suffered from the Depression between the two wars. But because of its dependence upon distributive trades and service industries, more than upon heavy industry, it suffered less than most; in the worst period of the Depression unemployment in York was approximately one half the national level.

The population went on steadily rising. In 1901 it had been 77,914. By 1931 it was 84,813. Despite the Second World War, by 1951 it reached 105,000, and grew to about 106,000 in the next decade.

On the eve of the Second World War, York was a city not fundamentally different from that of the nineteenth century. But it was a city that had significantly spread its boundaries and changed, not so much in the centre as in the housing areas surrounding the city and the roads immediately outside its walls. The built-up area, once less than 300 acres in extent, had increased to about 1,800 acres by 1882; by the end of the Second World War it had increased to over 6,000 acres. The big housing developments, first in the Groves to the north, then in Tang Hall to the east, then at Acomb in the west, had begun to give

York a new kind of character—with low density housing, plenty of grass and trees, and two-storey brick houses, many of them semi-detached.

The best of the houses were still outside the boundaries of the city at New Earswick, Joseph Rowntree's model garden village. There were also extensions on the Rowntrees' estate at Clifton. The brick and tile houses, mostly detached, with large gardens thickly planted with trees and shrubs, were designed by Barry Parker, who had also designed the houses in New Earswick. They had some of the first 'through' living rooms, allowing the same type to be orientated in different ways. They had big gardens and outhouses and were in many ways model dwellings for the middle class areas beginning to push the city out to the west and south.

The Second World War was a turning point for most towns and cities in Great Britain, not so much because of war damage (York suffered relatively little from a bombing raid which demolished the church of St Martin le Grand and completely gutted the Guildhall in the centre of the city) as because of the reports and legislation concerning housing and planning that accompanied and followed it. The Town and Country Planning Act of 1947 transformed the system of development. By that time, York—like most other cities—had commissioned an Advisory Plan. It was published in 1948 and is worth discussion because of the picture it gives of York in mid-century, about to change.

It noted that the population at the end of the Second World War was estimated at 102,340 and that the area of the city was 6,450 acres. It followed the current planning fashion of recommending primary use zones and emphasized the problem of traffic. Advice from central government and local surveys had revealed that there was a serious increase of traffic, particularly on the main route from the south-west to the north-east, the old Roman route which came from Tadcaster, went out towards Malton and passed through the centre via the station, Lendal Bridge, Deangate (built in 1903) and Good-ramgate.

In the light of subsequent events it is remarkable how many of them were contained in the Advisory Plan. Its authors considered that a bridge should be built across the Ouse at Water End in Clifton. The bridge, ultimately built in the early 1960s, acts as a link between suburban areas and not in any way as a by-pass to the city. To provide that, the authors of the report recommended that a new Outer Ring Road should be built further away from the built-up area of the city, beyond Skelton village on the north, beyond Naburn village on the south.

Internally there should be a new Inner Ring Road around the mediaeval walls. It was not however to be close to those walls, following the roads developed immediately outside them, mainly in the nineteenth century. It was to be approximately 250 yards away from the walls, to be a dual-carriageway and to be set in a green belt which would provide public open space within sight of the walls and an incomparable view of the walls themselves.

104

Within the walled area certain streets, such as Stonegate and Shambles, should be closed to all wheeled traffic after 10 o'clock in the morning—a proposal which was only to be brought within practical possibility over twenty years later. A reasonable route from east to west through the centre of the city was already more or less in existence in the form of the route through Blake Street, Daveygate, Parliament Street and Piccadilly. What was now needed was an improved route through the middle of the city from the south-west to the north-east, on the main line of the traffic through the city but avoiding Deangate and the roads close to the Minster, which were in any case too narrow and not appropriate for widening. To that end the Plan proposed the new road which was in due course built—Stonebow, linking the end of Micklegate and High Ousegate to Peaseholme Green and ultimately to the Malton road. Parliament Street, with its famous weekly market in the middle of the road, was to become a roadway again with parking for cars; and a new market was to be created in the area between Parliament Street and Shambles. On the other hand certain roads should be kept exactly as they were—for instance, Petergate, Colliergate, Fossgate, Stonegate, Great Shambles and St Saviourgate.

The official development plan for the city was published in the form of a survey in 1951 and the plan itself in 1956. It incorporated most of the earlier proposals and provided a framework for the development of the city in the next decades. It also reiterated some basic principles, insisting, for example, that 'If the character of old York is to be retained—and this is the intention of the Planning Authority—traffic difficulties in the city centre cannot be resolved by schemes for extensive road widening.' It concluded that links were needed through the areas behind the major streets so that building frontages on those streets would not be affected, and that a solution must be found to the central area by diverting non-stopping traffic. The plan also took note of the fact that approximately 15,000 bicycles a day pass the intersection of the A64 and the A19 in the middle of the city.

In the light of those plans it is disappointing that the actual development that took place during the fifties and sixties fell far short of the admirable intentions expressed in them. Some of the housing, mainly in the areas described earlier, was good and even imaginative; the Walmgate slum clearance area, for example, though unfashionable now, was adventurous for its time. But most of the new buildings were mundane and without character. The new road in the centre where the Hungate area had been cleared, Stonebow, was clumsily defined and framed by commercial properties that would have disgraced any town, let alone one with the historic importance of York. Faced with confusing evidence, from the certainty of the advisory plan to the hesitance and inconsistency of the planning permission given by the authority, architects seem to have sought refuge in a faceless brick and concrete style of no certain provenance that would hopefully upset the existing state of things as little as possible. The result was to upset it very greatly, substituting for sound old houses in the city centre some banal constructions that began to erode the character of the city.

Nor was the standard of design much better in the outlying areas. The Tang Hall estate was already mostly complete. The area to the west, Acomb, now expanded rapidly, housing eventually as many people as the whole of the mediaeval city. It had none of its character, nor indeed much character at all. The houses by speculative builders were as uninteresting, in layout and design, as such developments usually are; they would not have been remarkable in any other town or city. The local authority housing was little better, bleakly laid out along tedious streets with little punctuation or any attempt at social planning of the kind which had so keenly distinguished the garden village of New Earswick or the local authority's own housing at Tang Hall before the war.

But if the general environment appeared to be deteriorating, some important changes were taking place which were in a short time to have a fundamental effect upon the physical fabric of the city and its social and economic life.

On 18 July 1946 the York Civic Trust had been founded—for the purpose of preserving the city's monuments and treasures and developing its beauties. Its terms of reference included everything which might profit the history, the beauty, the reputation and the happiness of York whether of its outward scene or of its cultural life. Its objects were 'To preserve for the benefit of the public the amenities of the City and neighbourhood, to protect from dilapidation, disfigurement or destruction, buildings and open spaces of beauty or historic interest; to acquire land or buildings for that purpose, to hold or develop them themselves, or to hand them over to the City, or to the nation; to encourage good design and craftsmanship in new erections and to create new beauty within or without the Walls.'

The Civic Trust was therefore immediately involved in problems of preservation, amenity and design. The cleaning up of buildings in the city, the provision of suitable additions to street scenes, the erection of plaques on buildings to record the life and activities of the people who had inhabited them, the painting of monuments and their lighting—these are examples of the work in which the Civic Trust engaged. More fundamental was the impact it was to have on the city's intellectual, cultural and social life.

From the start, the Civic Trust formed an Academic Development Committee with the intention of fostering a university in the City of York and pledged its support to any attempt to found a university or university college. It made two immediate experiments. The first was the Borthwick Institute of Historical Research, placed in St Anthony's Hall, one of the late mediaeval guildhalls within the city walls—a collection of diocesan and provincial archives deposited there by the Church and extended significantly as a result of endowments. The second was the formation in St John's Church, Micklegate, a mediaeval parish church then derelict and scheduled for demolition, of the Institute of Advanced Architectural Studies. The purpose of this Institute was at first to supply courses for architects on the protection and repair of historic buildings; to those were later added many other courses, particularly on the management and technology of architecture and building for architects, planners and builders. The two academic institutes formed the nucleus of what was to become the University of York.

In April 1960 approval was given for the establishment of the University of York. A year later Robert Matthew, Johnson-Marshall and Partners were appointed development architects and in January 1962 the first Vice Chancellor, Lord James of Rusholme, and the first members of the academic staff of the new University arrived in York. The first students arrived in October 1963. The development plans envisaged a university of some 3,000 students, developed over a period of approximately ten years. Its main site, meeting the requirements of government, was of nearly 200 acres at Heslington Hall to the immediate south-east of the city boundary. It was planned as a comprehensive academic community with some emphasis upon the social sciences as well as upon the basic sciences and the arts.

Central to its concept was the proposal that it should be a collegiate university—a community of eight colleges, each offering not only academic facilities but residence and social facilities as well. The University emerged as a continuous development of informally grouped buildings, constructed in a prefabricated system of building known as CLASP, gradually reaching away from Heslington Hall towards the city and filling the major part of the site.

The site was already partially landscaped. Its landscaping now became a principal feature of the new development. Hundreds of trees were planted; the land was recontoured and drained so as to form a huge lake, twisting through the middle of the site and providing a visual unity for the various university buildings. Within an astonishingly short period the University of York was able to present an apparently mature landscape with buildings and shrubs and grass, animals and birds and fish—as well as staff and students.

Back in the city centre, the university had a less obvious but important effect upon the life and fabric of the city. It already had the old buildings of the two Institutes, now postgraduate institutes of the university. It acquired, in addition, Micklegate House, one of the mid-eighteenth century mansions on the great street, and subsequently the buildings next to it. Furthermore, in order to enable the university to make an earlier start than would otherwise have been possible, the Corporation leased to it the buildings of the King's Manor, which it had recently acquired. The King's Manor was extensively restored and became the nucleus for the start of the university. Then, as the main departments and the whole of the undergraduate teaching moved out to Heslington, the King's Manor became the university's headquarters in the centre of York. The Architectural Institute was moved there from St John's Church, to be joined by researchers in modern languages and language teaching, and mediaeval art, including stained glass.

The university brought not only restoration to ancient buildings, it also provided a major new departure in the economic life of the city. The centre of law and lunacy was now also a centre of learning. To it came staff and students, admirers as well as critics and commentators upon the state of the city and on its development. Since I was myself one of them and since I rapidly became involved in discussions and controversies about those matters, it seems reasonable to introduce some personal comments about the York that I then encountered.

The city that I began to explore on foot in the early 1960s was a York already scarred by modern intrusions, displaying a remarkable lack of scholarship and an equally remarkable vulgarity. Nevertheless those intrusions were still on a relatively small scale. The city as a whole was still an experience of profound human interest and intervals of beauty.

In contrast to the new environment being created after the bombing in other cities and towns, in contrast also to the major set pieces of architectural history, York offered not major monuments, vistas and grand symmetrical exercises, but an idiosyncratic mixture of things on a small and human scale. George Pace, in a paper entitled *The York Aesthetic*, pointed out at that time that 'in York there are very few individual buildings of outstanding architectural worth'; but he added, 'Minster, churches, chapels, ruins, assembly rooms, Mansion House, public buildings, shops and houses, all cheek by jowl, all bounded and enclosed by the Bar walls and gates, produce a city having an Aesthetic very much greater than the sum of the parts and unsurpassed in this land.'

Pace identified certain fundamental aspects of that Aesthetic—propinquity, contrast, high drama, muted drama, even vulgarity and insipidness. With that study as a reference, I began to carry out the same exercise and to elaborate it further, in an attempt to describe for myself the character of York.

The city centre of York is particularly characterized by the overlaying of one historical period upon another. Not in big areas, but by the juxtaposition of buildings very closely one with another. Those buildings are tightly grouped and close-packed. That involves in turn the mixture of uses; in contrast with the contemporary policy of separating primary use zones and identifying certain areas of one major function in contrast with certain areas of another, the characteristic of the streets of York is that functions are closely jammed together and conflicting uses exist side by side.

Those uses are small in scale. The close-packed grouping of buildings results in irregularity and the lack of a coherent style; the mixture of periods as well as building types means that no overall architectural style is evident. There is no symmetry in the street scene, even if there is a symmetrical building. There are no straight axes, all groupings are informal. This even includes Georgian developments which in other cities such as

Edinburgh, Bath and London, tend to be symmetrical, formal and large-scale; in contrast with them, the Georgian developments of York are isolated and intermingled with the buildings of other periods.

The juxtaposition of one building type with another can most easily be seen at street corners, a junction often made with brutality and suddenness. The same disregard for neat and gentle links between things can be seen at the riverside; elevations drop sheer into the water at the side of the Ouse. The character of the street-scapes is created by minor buildings rather than major ones. It depends upon broken sight-lines and broken profiles; it also depends upon a variegated silhouette. And with that goes a mixture of materials— brick, limestone, slates, pantiles, timber and rendering—all of it in marked contrast with the characteristic materials as well as formal groupings of modern buildings. Oddly, the city appeared to have turned its back on the river. The rear elevation of Woolworths in Coney Street was a tangle of drainpipes and patched brickwork rising in outrageous indecency above the Ouse near Ouse Bridge. On the other hand, near it was an untidy collection of backyards with trees and shrubs and derelict sheds, also framing the river, which seemed in some other way to be typical of York.

York seemed almost to need a certain amount of dirt. One of its characteristics was an off-hand acceptance, almost a disregard, for priceless antiquities. It seemed happy to turn its back, not only on the river frontage, but, in places like Gillygate, also on the mediaeval wall. The land at the east end of the Abbey ruins, one of the most spectacular architectural sites in the country, was at that time a tangle of grass, unkempt and disregarded. York was like the backyard of England and that was one of its attractions.

If so, those idiosyncracies existed in almost direct conflict with the tendencies and trends of the modern city. Those trends, towards bigger buildings, wider streets, new shop fronts, the use of new materials and the reorganization of street areas, all found the old York an impediment. By the end of the sixties, as amenity societies began everywhere to flourish and the issue of conservation became a national preoccupation, York began to attract the attention of the nation as a whole and the problems of conservation and the preservation of the historic fabric of the city became of prime importance.

It already had an unusual number of buildings listed as being of architectural and historical importance. As a result of further work during the 1960s York found itself with 850 listed buildings, of which 650 were inside the walls. By then it also had some unfortunate additions, notably those in Rougier Street (large blocks of standard, faceless offices), in Stonebow (a rather more aggressive block of offices and shops), St Saviourgate (another faceless office block at one end of a small-scale street), in Goodramgate (where a new supermarket was disguised as if it were part of a row of smaller shops) and in Market Street (perhaps the most extraordinary manifestation, where a two-storey shop was given a three-storey façade with an empty top floor looking as if it had been bombed).

The Precinct

Such new buildings precisely represented the problem of an old city faced with new demands. Those demands were for offices on a much bigger scale, repetitive, with floor above floor of identical accommodation, in contrast with the old buildings which they were replacing or attempting to use; they were also for shops which now required large spaces open on the ground floor with some further shopping space or storage on the first floor with nothing above. To both of those demands the old houses in the historic streets of York provided an irrelevant answer. The natural outcome was therefore to demolish such buildings, or at least alter them in such a way that their old façades were meaningless in relation to the internal activities of the building.

York therefore, in the sixties, was a classic case of the conflict between preservation and development. On the one hand there was an increasing number of tourists following a trail that led between the Minster and the castle. On the other hand there was the development of York as a regional and local shopping centre. That centre was approximately in a square bounded by Parliament Street, High Ousegate, Coney Street and St Helen's Square—an area already badly eroded by inadequate modern buildings. But underneath it all, the question posed was what kind of place York was to be. Was it to be a regional centre for offices and shopping and cultural activities? If so their needs were in conflict with the preservation of the old, obsolete historic fabric.

In this York was not alone. Its problems were much the same as those of most other historic cities. In an attempt to answer the questions the government in 1966 nominated four cities for studies in conservation; that is, not just preservation, but preservation and enhancement in the interests of the community. The study of York was carried out by Lord Esher, architect and planner, and published as *York: a Study in Conservation* in 1968. It captured the imagination of the city and established York as a test case for conservation as a whole.

Lord Esher's team noted all the usual problems of an historic city—the influence of motor traffic and parking inside the walls, the effects of commercial pressures on the city centre, the conflict with the preservation of listed buildings, the inherent problems of the economics of restoration and maintenance, the need to improve the environment, to control new development and to study the total cost of conservation. They also made some important factual discoveries. Whereas 10,000 people, approximately, had lived within the city walls in the Middle Ages, now only 3,500 people were living there. Within the walls were one and a half million square feet of shopping space; there were 3,500 workers (mostly shopworkers) and 7,500 office workers. There were also nearly two and a half million square feet of industry and warehousing, and—a figure shortly to be exceeded—there were a million visitors a year.

In a brilliant summary of the history of the fabric of the city, the consultants isolated certain themes fundamental to the changing nature of the city. Inherent in its modern problems was the ebbing of fashionable life in the early nineteenth century and the replacement of the old buildings and the spaces associated with them by backyard manufactures. The historic core had become a working place rather than a living place. The gardens and orchards of the mediaeval city had been replaced by the yards and sheds of the Victorian city, with workshops set against the big houses. With the moving of people into the suburbs the houses became shops on the ground floor and storage above. Since most of the older street houses are three or four storeys in height, a huge area of floor space—estimated at 40 per cent of the total—in the central area was now unused.

The result was urban blight at all stages of that phenomenon; it could be seen in ancient streets like Micklegate, where the building of stores had led to the widening of the street, or St Andrewgate, which was virtually derelict. Of the twelve finest town houses, only three had any sort of back garden left. The general scene was one of empty buildings or—more often—of empty upper floors, of ramshackle conversions to unsuitable uses and of façades hiding new uses and less admirable buildings behind.

Lord Esher's Report laid down five objectives, which seemed reasonable for any historic city and appropriate for York. They were:

1. That the commercial heart of York should remain alive and able to compete on level terms with its neighbour cities, new or old.
2. That the environment should be so improved by the elimination of decay, congestion and noise that the centre will become highly attractive as a place to live in for families, for students and single persons, and for the retired.
3. That land uses which conflict with these purposes should be progressively removed from the walled city.
4. That the historic character of York should be so enhanced and the best of its buildings so secured that they become economically self-conserving.
5. That within the walled city the erection of new buildings of anything but the highest architectural standard should cease.

To these ends various ingenious proposals were made. They included plans for new 'villages' within the walls at Bishophill and Aldwark, for some office development in the city centre, for hotels along the river, for the removal of cars from certain areas and the provision of four multi-storey car parks within five minutes walk of the centre of the city (defined as the original Thursday Market, St Sampson's Square). The maximum height for new buildings should be that of the top of the aisle roofs of the Minster.

The Conservation Study envisaged an 'inner enclave' in which some streets would be restricted to pedestrians, paved from wall to wall and closed to all vehicles from 10 a.m. to 5 a.m. the next morning; this would eventually spread to the rest of the shopping centre, including the 'restricted area' in which an electric trolley service would supply goods to the shops from a central goods depot on the Foss Islands industrial site. The four multi-storey car parks, with a total capacity of 5,000 cars, would provide for the needs of shoppers and office workers.

In short, the prospect was opened up of a mainly pedestrian precinct on a huge scale—nothing less than the greater part of the walled city. Here at one stroke was the possibility of solving York's basic problems and making a new and exciting unity of it. The city could be developed as a shopping centre; it could increase as a tourist attraction; and the possibility existed that it would all work economically.

Unfortunately, as in all planning situations, there were some fundamental problems. The first was that whatever the economic arguments for conservation, however the balance-sheet was drawn up (allowing, for example, for the re-use of the unused floors in the city centre), however great the attraction of the city in turning visitors into spenders, a coherent conservation policy required substantial central government aid. The second was the problem of traffic. Although traffic proposals for the intramural area were an integral part of the Esher study, his terms of reference precluded him from looking at traffic problems for the city as a whole. That may have been partly the reason for the inadequacy of his traffic proposals; it was in any case to become a focus of controversy.

For while Lord Esher was making his study of conservation, the city's officials were making a number of far-reaching studies and proposals for the reorganization of traffic in the city as a whole. In this they were influenced by the report on *Traffic in Towns*, a seminal study by Professor Colin Buchanan published in 1963, whose central arguments concerning accessibility, the definition of environmental areas and the need either to rebuild on a huge scale or seriously to restrict traffic in a city centre, were applied by the City to the situation in York.

Buchanan's Report made the point that with present and foreseeable increases in traffic (the number of vehicles rising from 10 million to 40 million within fifty years), towns and cities would be irreparably eroded unless either astronomical sums were spent on city centre redevelopment or action was taken to limit the number of vehicles using the central areas. One of his case studies was of Norwich, which has affinities with York. The application of the principles he announced would involve for York the creation of a 'primary distributor' road to take the bulk of the cross-town traffic, preferably just outside the walls. If then the intramural area was divided into 'environmental areas' reached from the primary distributor, the criss-cross traffic at present in the city centre would be diverted to the distributor, the environmental areas within the walls could be connected with each other only by foot, and the main part of the city centre could be pedestrianised, its ancient streets restored as footstreets.

In any case, the need for fundamental traffic studies was clear. Between 1945 and 1965 traffic nationally had increased fourfold. In York the increase had been similar; in the five years from 1960 to 1965 it increased by 20 per cent. Surveys by city officials had shown that the traffic followed certain well known patterns. For example, whereas nearly 40 per cent of the traffic approaching the city boundary from the south-west was in principle 'by-passable', only 17 per cent of that traffic was 'by-passable' if measured just outside the mediaeval walls at Micklegate. Over 80 per cent of the existing central area traffic, which would in any case increase, had to be accommodated unless it was to be banned from the city altogether.

The official studies and proposals to attack the traffic problems were published between 1967 and 1970. By that time it had been agreed that there should be a by-pass outside the city boundaries for traffic which at present has to pass through the city centre or immediately round the mediaeval walls on its way to the coast. The designation of footstreets was begun. Stonegate, the mainly mediaeval street in the centre on the line of the original Via Praetoria of the Roman legionary fortress, was closed to traffic for most of the day in 1971 and paved in 1975. In terms of shopping turnover and of amenity it was an immediate success. To take the traffic that surveys showed was the main load, that is the traffic that crossed the city itself, the Council approved the concept of an Inner Ring Road close to the walls, limited in width and capacity to a two-lane dual carriageway. They then commissioned consultants to report on the actual line of the road with proposals for landscaping. The report was published in March 1971.

Opposition, which had been minimal until then, was quickly organized; several groups were formed and controversy grew. It was inevitable that before long people would ask, no longer whether the line of the road was the right one, but whether an inner ring road was necessary at all. In that the protesters matched the growing national mood. By the time an enquiry was held, in the autumn of 1972, every kind of objection and all kinds of alternative proposals had been voiced. Correspondents to the local paper proved that no road was necessary, one senior academic even urging people to go to Oxford to see how the traffic problems had been solved! The enquiry itself lasted seven weeks.

To the planners it seemed that at least two policies were essential. First, it was desirable that much of the city centre should be made into pedestrian areas, so that people could shop and look around in the old streets; and this would not be impossible because the area inside the walls is relatively small. Given car parks in key places, everywhere in the centre could be accessible on foot within a few minutes. Given a simple system of baskets on wheels (such as some of the new shopping centres are providing) which could be left at the car parks, shopping could be nearly as easy as in a modern out-of-town shopping centre, and much more pleasurable.

Secondly, there must be a good, quick and efficient means of access to the walled area, for dwellers, workers, shoppers and others, so that the city centre would be a thriving and desirable place to use. Hence the general position of the proposed Inner Ring

Road—theoretically located just outside the historic walls, thus following a Buchanan suggestion of finding the crack between the central area and the area with the main residential and industrial uses.

In a predominantly Victorian city such as Leeds this crack is almost certain to be in the 'inner ring' of substandard housing that surrounded the old core when the railway or the canal arrived and houses were hurriedly thrown up to accommodate as many workers as possible within walking distance of the works and the communications. In such a case the provision of a new inner ring road can be usefully combined with the demolition and replacement of thousands of unfit houses, such as the back-to-backs.

In the case of a city like York the geographic situation was not so simple. As in other cities, there are unfit and bye-law houses just inside and just outside the mediaeval walls, and the proposed Ring Road took the opportunity to remove some of the latter. But there are other stretches in York where such houses do not occupy the line of the proposed road and where there are aesthetic and historic reasons why difficulties should occur.

In the event, the inspector at the public enquiry found in favour of the ring road, and the Secretary of State for the Environment, after considering the problem for two years, overruled the inspector's recommendation and found against it. The road as proposed will therefore not be built in the near future. The pedestrian area has been extended and there are more foot-streets, without the ring road.

What was fascinating as a reflection of the character of York was the intensity of feeling which the controversy revealed. People felt very passionately about the city and about its future. The ring road was much hated. But the traffic problem was not solved. Perhaps it was incapable of solution.

The controversy also revealed a more fundamental problem. Proposals had been made to build an out-of-town shopping centre at Huntingdon, north of York, and another possibly west of York as well. Such a centre, with ready access and car parking and convenient movement between shops and supermarkets would have a serious effect upon the commercial centre of York.

On the other hand, perhaps that centre could become residential again. To that end proposals have been made for the redevelopment of the Aldwark district, just inside the city walls near Monk Bar and partially derelict—one of the areas where handsome Georgian houses such as Peaseholme House were converted into workshops and where formerly smart residential streets have declined into a collection of yards and backlands. The removal of a brewery from the area enabled the Civic Trust to make plans for the restoration of houses. It restored and let for residential use a good Georgian house on the street; it announced plans for the complete—and expensive—restoration of Peaseholme House. At the same time, with the help of substantial government grant, a realistic project was devised for the total rehabilitation of the area. Aldwark thus becomes a test case;

can York afford—and will people pay—to convert an intramural area back to residential use?

In any case, both Lord Esher and the City Planning Office made proposals for the establishment of a Conservation Area, that is, an area defined under the Civic Amenities Act of 1967 in which it is desirable both to preserve and enhance the buildings and their environment. Esher drew the boundaries of the conservation area fairly tightly; the city drew them more broadly and designated a more comprehensive area, later extending it and including other areas as well. But essentially both included a substantial proportion of the intramural city, including the whole of Roman York and most of Danish and mediaeval York on the left bank of the river, together with a line of buildings on both sides of Micklegate and most of Blossom Street on the right bank. The conservation area thus extended outside the walls.

But the establishment of a conservation area immediately poses another question. If so high a proportion of the central area of the city can be designated for conservation, and if that area includes sub-standard pieces of the environment as well as admirable historical examples, in what way is a conservation area in York different from York itself? Could not the whole city be designated as a conservation area, worth preserving and enhancing? Conservation, after all, is not essentially different from good planning; and good planning in a city like York must involve preservation. It must also involve a conflict between the demands of economics and the demands of preservation.

Meantime the problem of the future of York as a regional shopping centre was intensified by a decision of the Secretary of State for the Environment, after a seven-day public enquiry, to approve the proposal for a hypermarket at Huntingdon, despite the opposition of the City Council and the Chamber of Trade. The developers claimed that its building would help to solve the city's traffic problems and leave the city centre a pleasanter place for tourists.

In saying that, they were making—perhaps unconsciously, perhaps not—a judgement about the future of the city as a whole. They were saying in effect that York's future was not as a major regional shopping centre or even a major commercial centre of any kind. Its future lay with tourism.

For what is happening to the city centre? The York Civic Trust, having brilliantly and successfully converted one of the redundant churches, St Sampson's, into a centre for elderly people, has, in collaboration with the City, converted another of the city's eleven redundant churches—St Mary's, Castlegate—into an information and exhibition centre for the understanding of the city, for the tourist guides, for meetings and for permanent displays of the city's history. Located close to the Castle Museum and Clifford's Tower it is directly on the tourist track. Its success is certain. The city having appointed a Director of Tourism and entered wholeheartedly into the promotion of the tourist industry, York has already become one of the main sites in England for visitors. The restoration of the Minster, the cleaning of both its interior and exterior and the provision of a new crypt beneath its central tower with a permanent display of the history and restoration of the Minster, has hugely increased the number of visitors. York is firmly established on the tourist circuit.

York thus stands at a crossroads. So it always has; for that is why it was located where it is in the first place. But now it is a crossroads in urban history. Almost uniquely preserved —as much by lethargy as until recently by conviction—and unusually attractive as a place for living as well as working, it could discover its true role. The reorganization of local government has left it a minor centre, not the headquarters of a county, as it had hoped to be. Perhaps therefore its future is as a tourist delight—with its Minster, its castle, its museums, its university, its guildhalls, its churches and its mansions: with a river improved and landscaped: with a new outdoor museum: with its hospitals and asylums and schools and incomparable public houses. And perhaps that would be most appropriate— more so than the future its leaders recently envisaged for it, as a thriving regional centre, prosperous and vital, economically self-conserving. For York has the whole of history built into its fabric. It may be most rewarding to those who live there not so much with an eye on its future as with an absorbing passion for its past.

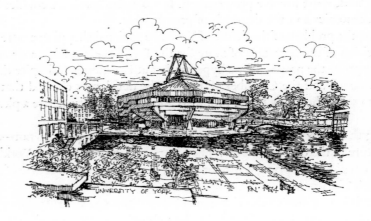

UNIVERSITY OF YORK

Maps

1   Roman York (*Chapter 1: The Legionary Fortress*)

2   Anglo-Danish York (*Chapter 2: The Market*)

3   Mediaeval York (*Chapter 3: Motte and Minster*)

4   Georgian York (*Chapter 5: Assembly Rooms*)

5   Nineteenth-Century York (*Chapter 6: Railway Street*)

6   Modern York (*Chapter 7: The Precinct*)

ROMAN YORK

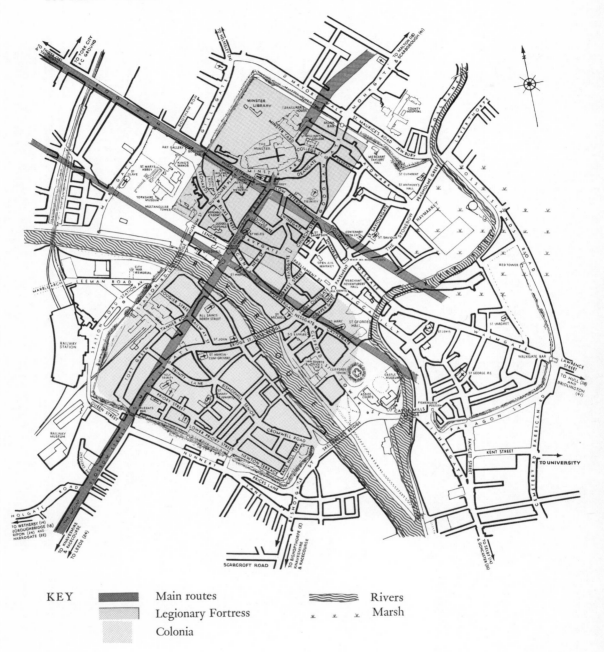

KEY

	Main routes
	Legionary Fortress
	Colonia

Rivers

Marsh

ANGLO-DANISH YORK

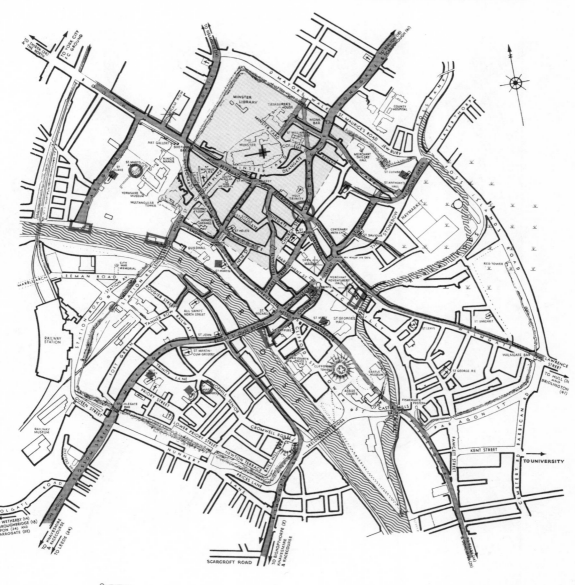

KEY

 Remains of Legionary Fortress

 Main routes

Palaces

Landing stages

Main markets

Pre-Norman Conquest churches

Norman Conquest castles

Rivers

Marsh

MEDIAEVAL YORK

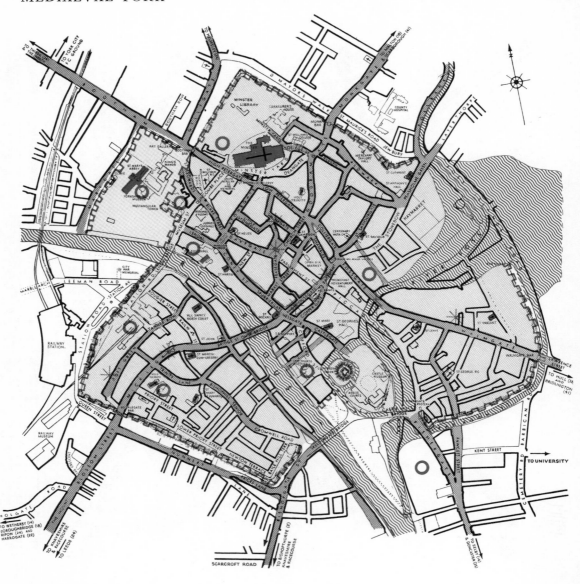

KEY

Area of Mediaeval York		Markets
Abbey Precinct		Religious houses
Mediaeval Wall		Churches
Rivers, fishponds and moats		Castle
Main routes		

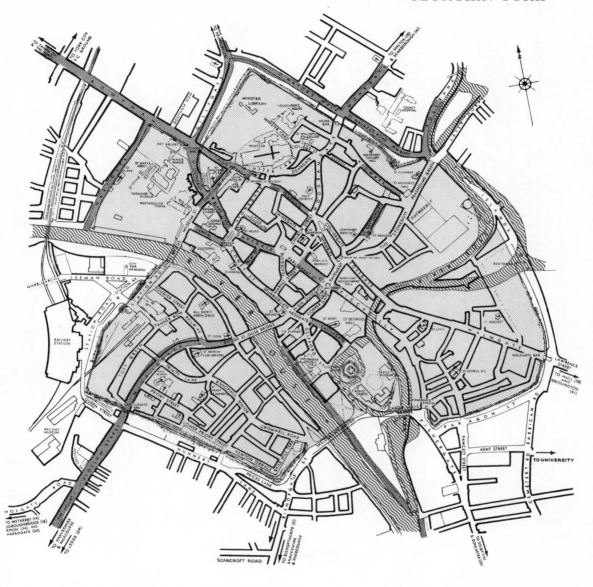

GEORGIAN YORK

KEY
Area of Mediaeval York
New streets or rebuilt streets
Rivers and islands

NINETEENTH-CENTURY YORK

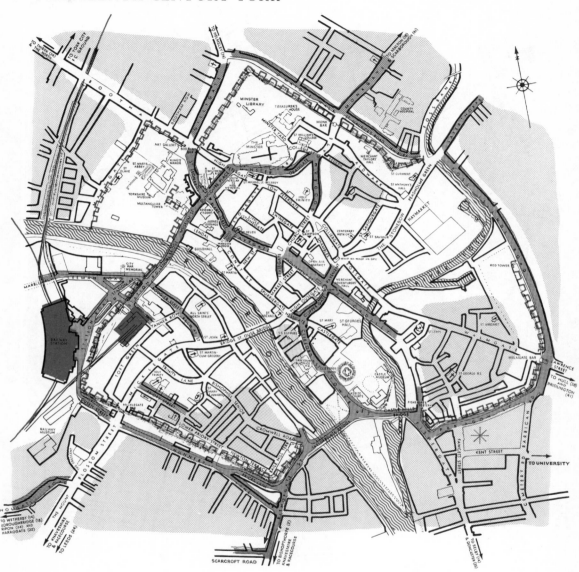

KEY

New roads

Rivers

Railway stations

Main areas of new housing

New cattle market

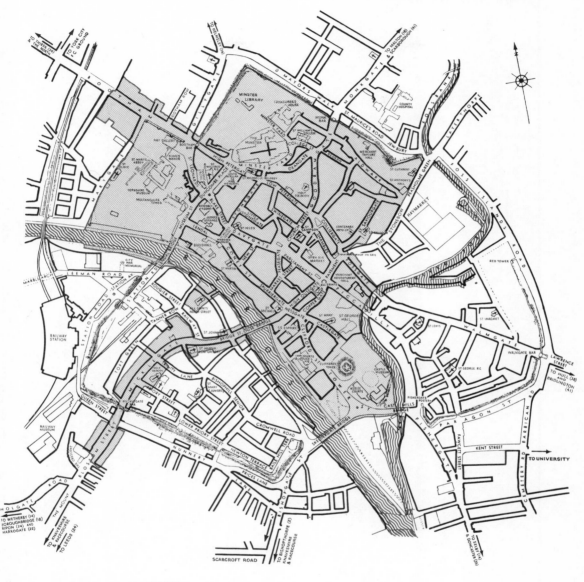

MODERN YORK

KEY Conservation Area

Bibliographical Note

Fundamental to any study of York is Francis Drake's *Eboracum* of 1736. Also essential is C. B. Knight's *A History of the City of York* of 1944, which is a detailed catalogue of events and personalities, year by year, the Victoria County History's *The City of York* of 1961 and the three volumes produced by the York office of the Royal Commission on Historic Monuments between 1962 and 1972. There are more to come, a welcome and essential contribution after a period of silence. Volume III, on *York South-West of the Ouse* (1972) contains (pp xxix–xxxvi) an invaluable account by John Harvey of Authorities, including lists and comments on Antiquaries and Historians, Artists and Surveyors, and Plans of York. The following bibliography does not contain current guide-books, pamphlets on individual buildings or articles in journals; I have however listed the principal journals which I have repeatedly consulted. Nor does it contain general works on English history, geography and architecture; it is confined to books that deal in significant measure specifically with York.

ADSHEAD, S. D., MINTER, C. J., NEEDHAM, C. W. C., *York, A Plan for Progress and Preservation*, York, 1948

BAINES, Edward, *History, Directory and Gazetteer of the County of York*, 1822–3

BENSON, G., *An Account of the City and County of the City of York: from the Reformation to the Year 1925*, York, 1925. Reprint 1968

BRITISH ASSOCIATION, *York: A survey*, York, 1959

BROCKBANK, J. L. and HOLMES, W. M., *York in English History*, London, 1909

BRUNSKILL, Elizabeth, *The York Mystery Plays*, York, 1963

BUTLER, R. M. (ed.), *Soldier and Civilian in Roman Yorkshire*, Leicester University Press, 1971

Bibliographical Note

CRAMP, Rosemary, *Anglian and Viking York*, (Borthwick Papers No. 33), York, 1967

COUNCIL FOR BRITISH ARCHAEOLOGY, *Research Report 7. Rural Settlement in Roman Britain*, London, 1966

DAVIES, Robert and SKAIFE, R. H., *Walks through the City of York*, London, 1880

DRAKE, Francis, *Eboracum: or the History and Antiquities of the City of York*, 1736

ESHER, Viscount, *York, A Study in Conservation* (Report to the Minister of Housing and Local Government and York City Council), H.M.S.O., 1968

FIFE, Michael and WALLS, Peter, *The River Foss—its History and Natural History*, York, 1973

HARGROVE, William, *New Guide for Strangers and Residents in the City of York*, 1838, (Republished, Wakefield 1971)

HARGROVE, W., *History and Description of the Ancient City of York*, 2 volumes, York, 1818

HUTTON, Barbara, *Clifton and its People*, York, 1969

KNIGHT, C. B., *A History of the City of York*, York, 1944

KNOWLES, John A., *The York School of Glass Painting*, London, 1936

MORRELL, J. B., *The City of Our Dreams*, London, 1940

MORRELL, J. B. and WATSON, A. P., *How York Governs Itself*, London, 1928

MORRIS, J. E., *York*, London, 1924

NICHOLL, Donald, *Thurstan, Archbishop of York*, York, 1964

NUTTGENS, P., *York* (City Buildings Series), London, 1970

PEARSON, F. R., *Roman Yorkshire*, London, 1936

PRESSLY, I. P., *A York Miscellany*, York, 1938, 1965

RADLEY, J., 'Economic Aspects of Anglo-Danish York', *Mediaeval Archeology*, Vol. 15 1971

RADLEY, J. and SIMMS, C., *Yorkshire Flooding—Some Effects on Man and Nature*, York, 1970

RAINE, A., *Mediaeval York*, London, 1955

RICHARDSON, Harold, *A History of Acomb*, York, 1963

RICHMOND, Ian, *York from its Origins until the Close of the 11th century* (Sheldon Memorial Lecture), York, 1959

ROCK'S VIEWS OF YORK 1852–1861, Leeds, 1971

ROWNTREE, B. Seebohm, *Poverty, a Study of Town Life*, London, 1901

ROWNTREE, B. Seebohm, *Portrait of a City's Housing* (Rebuilding Britain Series), London, 1945

ROYAL COMMISSION ON HISTORICAL MONUMENTS, *An Inventory of the Historical Monuments in the City of York*, Vol. I Eburacum: Roman York, H.M.S.O., 1962; Vol. II The Defences, H.M.S.O., 1973; Vol. III South-West of the Ouse, H.M.S.O., 1972

SESSIONS, W. K. and E. MARGARET, *The Tukes of York in the Seventeenth, Eighteenth and Nineteenth Centuries*, York, 1971

SPENCE, M. and EVERATT, M., *A Short History of York*, London, 1948

STACPOOLE, Alberic (ed.), *The Noble City of York*, York, 1972

STAPLETON, H. E. C. and THOMPSON, M. J. A., *Skelton Village*, York, 1971

VICTORIA COUNTY HISTORY OF THE COUNTY OF YORK, *The City of York*, ed. P. M. Tillott, O.U.P., 1961

WENHAM, L. P., *Eboracum* (Ginn History Patch Series: The Romans), London, 1970; *The Great and Close Siege of York 1644*, Kineton, 1970; *York*, London, 1971

WIDDRINGTON, Sir Thomas, *Analecta Eboracensia*, (ed. Caesar Caine), London, 1897

WILLIS, Ronald, *Nonconformist Chapels of York 1693–1840*, (York Georgian Society Occasional Paper No. 8), York, 1963; *Portrait of York*, London, 1972; *York as it was*, London, 1972

YORK ARCHAEOLOGICAL TRUST, *Interim Bulletins*, 1973 to date

YORK CITY COUNCIL, *Development Plan Survey*, 1951; *A Guide for Developers*, 1966; *Inner Ring Road Study*, 1967; *Report on Proposed Conservation Areas*, 1968; *Report on Parking*, 1969; *Central Area Traffic Scheme*, 1970

YORK CIVIC TRUST, *Annual Reports*, 1946 to date

YORK GEORGIAN SOCIETY, *The Works in Architecture of John Carr*, York, 1973; *Occasional Papers Nos. 1–8*; *Annual Reports*, 1944 to date

YORK GROUP FOR THE PROMOTION OF PLANNING, *The Strays and Ways of York*, York, 1968

YORK INSTITUTE OF ARCHITECTURAL STUDY, *Studies in Architectural History*, (ed. W. A. Singleton), Vol. I, 1954, Vol. II, 1956

YORK REDUNDANT CHURCHES COMMISSION, *New Uses for Old Churches*, York, 1967

YORK AND EAST YORKSHIRE ARCHITECTURAL SOCIETY, *Year Books*, especially 1956–7

YORKSHIRE ARCHAEOLOGICAL SOCIETY, *The Yorkshire Archaeological Journal Record Series*, Vols. 1–135, 1885–1973

YORKSHIRE ARCHITECTURAL AND ARCHAEOLOGICAL SOCIETY, *A Short Guide to Roman York*, 1962; *A Short Guide to the Roman Fortress at York*, 1968; *Roman York from A.D. 71*, 1971

YORKSHIRE PHILOSOPHICAL SOCIETY, *Annual Reports*, 1825–1973

Index

Abbot's House, 61, 62
Acomb, 81, 94, 95, 98, 102, 103, 106
Acomb House, 79, 80
Acomb Landing, 98
Agricola, 22
Aidan, 28, 29
Aire, River, 24, 83
Aire and Calder Navigation, 69, 75
Alcuin, 29
Aldborough (Isurium Brigantum), 21, 55
Aldwark, 78, 111, 114
All Saints, North Street, 14, 51, 56
All Saints, Pavement, 35, 37, 51, 77
Analecta Eboracensia, 66
Andrews, G. T., 95
Anglians, 28, 31, 36
Anglo-Saxons, 28, 45, 68
Ann Middleton's Hospital, 64, 77
Antonine Wall, 25
Archbishop's Palace, 32, 53, 63, 80
Aske, Robert, 57
Assembly Rooms, 67–83, 95
Assize Courts, 42, 70, 74, 81
Athelstan, 30
Atkinson, Peter, 75, 95
Augustinians, 46, 52
Aulus Plautius, 21

Back Lendal, 90
Baile Hill, 36, 38, 43
Bamburgh, 28
Bannockburn, Battle of, 47
Baptists, 80
Bar Convent, 80
Barclay's Bank, 96
Barden Tower, 46
Barker Hill, 91
Barton, 30
Bath, 72, 76, 109
Bay Horse, 14
Bayldon and Berry's, 83
Bearpark's Garden, 98
Bede, The Venerable, 29
Bedern, 53, 54, 91, 97, 102
Benedictines, 46, 51, 52, 59
Beningborough, Bourchiers of, 70, 87
Benson, Robert, 70
Berwick, 61
Beverley, 47
Bingley, Lord, 70
Birmingham, 68
Bishophill, 32, 37, 78, 92, 93, 111
Bishophill House, 97
Bishophill Senior, 62
Bishopthorpe, 63, 70, 80, 88

Index

Black Death, 50
Blake Street, 31, 72, 78, 105
Bloodaxe, Eric, 30
Blossom Street, 14, 65, 78, 93, 115
Blue Bridge, 75, 78
Bolton Castle, 46
Bootham, 36, 60, 63, 65, 73, 76, 78, 94, 96
Bootham Asylum, 80
Bootham Bar, 23, 44, 56, 80, 82, 93
Bootham Park Hospital, 80
Bootham School, 80
Bootham Stray, 55
Boroughbridge, 45
Borthwick Institute of Historical Research, 106
Bosworth, Battle of, 48
Botterill's Horse Repository, 100
Boudicca, 22
Bradford, 88
Bramham Park, 70
Brierley, W. H., 95, 96
Brigantes, 21, 22
Bristol, 48, 63, 68
Britannia Inferior, 24
British Association, 85
British Museum, 87
British Sugar Corporation, 103
Brittany, Count Alan of, 51
Brough, 21
Buchanan, Professor Colin, 112, 114
Buckingham House, 62, 79, 92
Burlington, Lord, Richard Boyle, 72, 73
Burton Stone Lane, 102
Burton Stone Public House, 95
Byland Abbey, 47, 60

Caer Ebrauc, 27
Caerleon, 22
Caernarvon, 43
Canute, 31
Carlisle, 61
Carlisle, Earl of, 70
Carmelites, 46, 52
Carr Dikes, 24
Carr Lane, 91

Carr, John, of York, 72, 73, 76, 78, 80, 81, 95
Carthusians, 46
Cartimandua, 21, 22
Castleford, 39
Castlegate, 40, 42, 54, 55, 78, 79, 81, 83, 91
Castlegate Ferry, 90
Castlegate House, 79, 81
Castlegate Postern, 82
Castlegate Postern Lane, 77
Castle Howard, 70, 81
Castle Mills, 44, 76, 87, 89
Castle Mills Bridge, 90, 98
Castle Museum, 42, 81, 115
Catterick, 21
Cavalry Barracks, 93, 96
Cawood, 45
Cemetery Road, 83, 94
Centenary Chapel, 80
Cerialis, Petilius, 22
Charlemagne, 29, 30
Charles I, 61, 63, 65, 97
Chester (Deva), 21, 22, 30, 35, 88
Cheviots, 21
Cistercian Abbeys, 45, 46
City Art Gallery, 16, 65, 98
City Library, 16
City Walls, 42
Civil War, 45, 60, 61, 64–68, 70, 81, 97
Classis Britannica, 20
Clementhorpe, 88, 93
Clifford Street, 92, 96, 98, 99
Clifford's Tower, 36, 42, 43, 53, 58, 92, 115
Clifton, 72, 81, 83, 94–96, 99, 102, 104
Coal Staith, 75
Colchester, 20, 21, 24
College Street, 53
Colliergate, 105
Colonia, 33, 37
Common Crane, 75
Coney Street, 32, 35, 77, 99, 109, 110
Conisborough Castle, 46
Connolly, William, 48
Constantine, 24
Constantius Chlorus, 24

Convent of Arden, 47
Conway, 43
Copmanthorpe, 85
Coppergate, 37, 88, 91
Corpus Christi Guild, 48, 50, 60
Cossin, 76, 79
Cotswolds, 21
Council Chamber, 48, 62, 99
Council Offices, 99
Council for Wales, 61
Council in the North, 60, 61, 62, 63
County Hospital, 80, 96
County Prison, 81
Coventry, 53
Crayke, 55
Cromwell, 65
Cumberland, 61
Cumberland House, 79

Dalton Terrace, 98
Darlington, 83, 86
Davygate, 77, 79, 91, 105
Davy Hall, 77
Dean Court, 95
Deangate, 91, 104, 105
Deanery, 53, 82
Debtors Prison, 42, 81
Defoe, Daniel, 70, 71, 73
Deira, 28
Denmark, 30, 31, 35
Devon, Earl of, 48
Dispensary, 73
Domesday, 33
Dominicans, 52, 76
Domus Palatina, 24
Doncaster, 28, 84, 86
Drake, Francis, 41, 66, 73, 74, 76, 77
Drake, Nathan, 78
Dredge, 89
Dringhouses, 94, 95
Dublin, 30, 35
Duncombe, Dean, 91
Duncombe Place, 77, 80, 91, 92, 96
Durham, 39, 61

Dutch River, 69
Dux Britanniarum, 23

Earlsborough, Earl's Palace, 35–37, 44, 51
Easingwold, 69
East Anglia, 30
East Riding, 28, 31
Eboracum, 20, 21, 22
Eboracum (Francis Drake), 73
Edinburgh, 76, 86, 109
Edward the Confessor, 33, 38, 41
Edward I, 43, 47
Edward II, 47
Edward III, 56
Edward IV, 47
Edwin, 28, 38, 52, 69
Edil, 34
Egbert, 29
Elm Bank Hotel, 95
Elmete, 28
Eoforwic, 28
Ermine Street, 46
Esher, Lord, 110–112, 115
Ethelburga, 28
Exeter, 41, 48, 63, 73

Fairfax House, 79, 81, 97
Farnese Palace, 95
Feasegate, 31, 34, 35
Festival Concert Rooms, 82
Ficteles Lane, 91
Finkle Street, 36, 91
Fishergate, 78, 87, 92
Fishergate Bar, 82, 92
Fishergate Postern, 36, 44
Fishergate Within, 92
Fishpool, King's, 40, 44, 65, 76, 87, 89, 92
Five Sisters, 53
Footless Lane, 91
Foss, The, 16, 17, 24, 31, 33–38, 40, 43, 45, 52, 54, 65, 75, 76, 78, 81, 87, 90, 92, 93, 98, 99
Foss Bridge, 48, 54, 64, 92
Foss Dike, 24
Fossgate, 44, 50, 64, 65, 98, 105

Index

Foss Islands, 86, 89, 99, 112
Foss Islands Road, 89
Foss Navigation, 43, 76, 89
Fosse Way, 21, 46
Foundry District, 94
Fountains Abbey, 46, 60
Fox, George, 80
Franciscans, 52, 56, 76, 91
Friargate, 80, 91
Fulford, 38, 78, 81, 94, 95, 96

Galtres, Forest of, 34, 55, 63, 68
Gargrave, Sir Thomas, 61
General Enclosure Act 1801, 68
General Post Office, 98
George Inn, 99
George Street, 92
George III, 68
Gillygate, 56, 65, 78, 91, 93, 109
Gloucester, 20, 21, 24
Godwin, Earl of Wessex, 38
Goldie, George, 95
Goodramgate, 31, 34, 52, 53, 55, 77, 91, 104, 109
Goole, 69
Goodricke, 73
Gough, 47
Grandstand, The, 72, 80
Grantham, 84
Grape Lane, 31
Gray's Court, 79
Great Fire, 78
Great North Road, 26, 47, 69
Great Northern Railway, 84
Great Shambles, 105
Green, Francis, 97
Gregory, Pope, 28, 32
Grosvenor Terrace, 96
Groves, The, 93, 103
Guild of Merchant Adventurers, 49
Guildhall, 48, 52, 57, 80, 99, 104
Guisborough, 47
Gyles, Henry, 59

Hadrian's Wall, 21, 25

Hagworm Nest, 97
Halfpenny, Joseph, 73
Halifax, 49, 63
Hansom, J. A., 92
Harewood Castle, 46
Hargrove, 74, 77, 91
Harold, 38
Harold Hardrada, King of Norway, 38
Harper, John, 95
Hastings, Battle of, 38
Hastings, Henry, Earl of Huntingdon, 61, 62
Hatfield, Battle of, 28
Hatfield Chase, 69
Haymarket, 74
Haxby, 94
Haxby Road, 88, 95, 96, 99
Helmsley Castle, 46
Helperby, 47
Henry IV, 47
Henry VII, 48, 61
Henry VIII, 59, 61, 62
Herbert House, 64
Heslington, 107
Heslington Hall, 107
Heslington Road, 94
Heworth, 94–96, 102
Hexham, 29
High Ousegate, 34, 35, 48, 105, 110
High Petergate, 78
Holgate, 86, 95, 102
Holgate, Robert, 61
Holgate Hill, 93
Holgate Road, 91, 94
Holtby, Richard, 62
Holy Trinity, Goodramgate, 51, 55
Holy Trinity Priory, 36, 52, 92
Honorius, 25
Hornby, 47
Horsefair, 53
Howard, Ebenezer, 99
Howden, 47
Hudson, George, 84, 85
Hudson Street, 24, 84
Hull, 49, 61, 63, 66, 92

Hull Road, 94
Humber, 20, 21, 26, 28, 30, 37, 38, 69
Hundred Years War, 47
Hungate, 102, 105
Huntingdon, 55, 94, 114

Iceland, 35
Icelandic Sagas, 34
Icknield Way, 46
Industrial Revolution, 49, 67, 68, 70, 97
Infantry Barracks, 93, 96
Ingram's Almshouses, 63
Ingram, Sir Arthur, 62, 63, 72
Inner Ring Road, 104, 113, 114
Institute of Advanced Architectural Studies, 13, 107
Ireland, 30, 97
Ironsides, 65
Isle of Man, 35
Ivar the Boneless, 30

Jacobites, 73
James, Lord, of Rusholme, 13, 107
Jarrow, 29
Jervaulx Abbey, 46, 60
Jews, 35, 43, 56
John, King, 47
Jones, George Fowler, 95
Jorvik, 30
Judea, 22
Judges' Lodgings, 79
Julius Caesar, 21

Kent, 21, 28, 30
King Street, 91
King's Manor, 13, 14, 59–66, 72, 73, 82, 96, 107
King's Mill, 65
King's Square, 23, 74
King's Staith, 35, 75, 79, 91
Kingsway, 103
Kirby, Edmund, 96
Kirkham Priory, 60
Kirkstall Abbey, 46
Knavesmire, 72, 73, 80, 94

Lady Row, 55
Lady Well, 78
Lancastrians, 47
Lastingham, 51
Law Courts, 99
Lawrence Street, 94, 96
Laycock, Dr, 102
Layerthorpe, 34, 94, 99, 102, 103
Layerthorpe Bridge, 45, 55, 65, 76, 90
Layerthorpe Postern, 44, 65
Leak and Thorp, 99
Leeds, 49, 63, 66, 68, 70, 75, 76, 81, 83, 88, 94, 114
Leeds Northern Railway, 86
Leeman Road, 90
Leeming, 47
Leetham, Henry, 87
Leetham's Mill, 95
Leicester, 20, 21
Lendal, 35, 55, 78, 79, 90, 98
Lendal Bridge, 35, 89, 90, 100, 104
Leslie, 65
Letchworth, 100
Lincoln, 20, 21, 22, 24, 73
Lindisfarne, 28, 29
Little Blake Street, 80, 91
Little Foss, 81
Liverpool, 68, 69
Llandaff, 61
Lodge, William, 65
London, 20, 46, 47, 50, 65, 68, 71, 72, 76, 78, 79, 81, 84–86, 93, 97, 109
Lop Lane, 54, 77, 91
Lord Mayor's Walk, 78, 91, 93
Lord President of the Council, 61, 63
Low Burton Hall, 46
Low Countries, 24, 30, 35
Low Ousegate, 77
Low Petergate, 78
Ludlow, 61
Lumley Castle, 46

Malet, William, 41
Malton (Derventio), 20, 21, 35, 36, 47, 52, 93, 104, 105

Index

Manchester (Manucium), 21, 25, 68, 88
Manor Shore, 83
Mansion House, 77, 79, 108
Marble Arch, 90, 94
Markenfield, 46
Markets, 77, 103
Market Street, 109
Market Weighton, 47
Marmoutier, Abbey of, 52
Marsden, Mr, 78
Marston Moor, Battle of, 65, 66
Martin, Jonathan, 82
Marygate, 35, 36, 51, 65, 73, 78
Marygate Estate, 94
Masham, 46
Mayne, James, 48
Mayor's Chamber, 48
Merchant Adventurers' Hall, 55, 57, 64
Methodists, 80, 96
Micklegate, 32, 34, 36, 52, 54, 55, 73, 74, 77–79, 84, 91, 105, 111, 113, 115
Micklegate Bar, 32, 44, 47, 56, 57, 65, 66, 73, 76, 82, 90
Micklegate House, 79, 87, 97, 107
Micklegate Stray, 55, 72
Middleham Castle, 46
Middlethorpe, 95
Middlethorpe Hall, 70
Middleton Colliery Railway, 83
Minster, 17, 23, 26, 28–31, 36–38, 40–58, 62–65, 71, 72, 79, 80, 90, 91, 95–97, 105, 108, 110, 111, 116
Minster Gates, 26, 53, 54
Minster Library, 53, 63
Minster Song School, 82
Monk Bar, 44, 56, 75, 76, 78, 82, 90, 114
Monk Bridge, 75
Monkgate, 52, 65, 78, 96
Monk Stray, 55
Moravians, 80
Morkere, 38
Mount, The, 76, 81, 93, 94, 96, 98
Mount Grace, 47
Mount Parade, 93

Mount Pleasant, 81, 93
Mount Vale, 81, 93
Mucky Pegg Lane, 91
Multangular Tower, 23, 101
Museum, The, 82, 95
Museum Gardens, 23, 36, 95
Museum Street, 90

Naburn, 20, 69, 76, 86, 87, 104
Navigation Road, 102
Nessgate, 35, 91
Newburgh, 47
Newcastle, 48
New Earswick, 14, 99, 104, 106
New Residence for the Canons Residentiary, 82
New Street, 77, 78, 83
New Walk, 73, 75, 78, 83, 99
Nonconformists, 80, 96
Norman Conquest, 27, 32, 36–38, 40–42, 46, 50, 51, 57, 87
North Eastern Railway, 86
North Riding, 88, 97
North Sea, 20, 24, 30
North Street, 44, 54, 56, 75, 84, 88, 90
Northallerton, 69
Northumberland, 47, 61
Northumberland, Earl of, 48
Northumbria, 30, 32, 38
Norway, 30, 31, 35, 38
Norwich, 41, 48, 63, 68, 88, 112
Nottingham, 65
Nowtgate, 92
Nunthorpe, 94

Ogleforth, 54
Oswald, Bishop, 32, 35
Oswald, King, 28
Ouse, River, 15, 16, 19, 20, 22, 24, 30–32, 34–36, 38–40, 43–45, 50, 54, 74–76, 78, 87, 89–91, 99, 100, 102, 104, 109
Ouse Bridge, 34, 35, 42, 48, 50, 54, 56, 59, 64, 75, 84, 89, 91, 109
Ousegate, 35, 37
Ouse Navigation, 69, 86

Outer Ring Road, 104
Oxford, 113

Pace, George, 108
Page, Thomas, 89
Palladianism, 72, 73
Parker, Barry, 100
Parliament, 66
Parliament Street, 82, 83, 93, 105, 110
Paulinus, 28
Pavement, 34, 37, 48, 64, 77, 79, 82, 91, 103
Peaseholme Green, 98, 103, 105
Peaseholme House, 97, 114
Peckitt, William, 73
Pennines, 21, 26, 69
Penty, W. G., 95
Percy, Sir Henry (Hotspur), 47
Peterborough, 84
Petergate, 23, 52, 53, 64, 65, 73, 79, 105
Peter's Prison, 53, 54
Pevensey, 38
Phoenix Foundry, 94
Piccadilly, 91, 94, 105
Pickering Castle, 46
Pilgrimage of Grace, 57, 59, 61
Place, Francis, 42, 73
Plumpton, Sir William, 47
Pocklington, 47
Police Station, 99
Pontefract Castle, 46
Poor Clares, 96
Poppleton, 86
Poppleton Road, 95, 96
Porta Decumana, 23
Porta Praetoria, 23, 24
Porta Principalis, 22
Porta Principalis Sinistra, 23
Precentor's Court, 79
Precentor's Lane, 79
Premonstratensians, 46
Presbyterians, 80, 96
Principia, 23
Priory Street, 92, 95, 96
Pritchett, J.P., 83, 95

Prosser, Thomas, 86
Public Library, 99
Purey Cust Nursing Home, 62

Quakers, 15, 80, 83, 96
Queen's Staith, 75, 87, 88
Queen Street, 86, 90

Railway Station, 95
Railway Street, 84, 85, 93, 100
Raimes and Company, 87
Ramsey, 32
Redfearn National Glass Company, 87
Red House, The, 79
Red Tower, 36, 44
Reformation, The, 59, 64, 92, 97
Regency York, 81
Restoration, The, 66–68, 74
Riccall, 38
Richard III, 48, 61
Richborough, 21
Richmond, 22
Richmond, Duke of, 61
Richmond, Professor, 24
Rievaulx Abbey, 46, 47, 60
Ripley Castle, 46
Ripon, 29, 46
Robert the Bruce, 47
Robert Matthew, Johnson-Marshall and Partners, 107
Rosary Street, 92
Rougier Street, 109
Rowntree's Cocoa Works, 83, 87, 88, 94, 99, 103, 104
Rowntree, Henry, 83, 88
Rowntree, Joseph, 99, 104
Rowntree, Joseph, Village Trust, 99
Rowntree, Seebohm, 97, 98
Royal Commission on Historical Monuments, 16
Royalists, 65
Rupert, Prince, 65

St Andrewgate, 79, 111
St Andrew's Priory, 83

Index

St Anthony's Hall, 57, 74, 106
St Augustine, 28
St Crux, 97
St Denys' Church, 92
St George's Church, 92, 96, 97
St Helen, 82
St Helen's Churchyard, 77
St Helen's Square, 83, 87, 95, 110
St John's, Ousebridge, 13, 51, 106, 108
St John's College, 95
St Leonards, 64, 74
St Leonards Crescent, 31
St Leonard's Hospital, 52, 59, 82
St Leonard's Place, 44, 78, 82, 93, 95
St Leonard's Tower, 98
St Margaret's Church, 92, 97
St Martin-cum-Gregory, 50, 51, 80
St Martin le Grand, 104
St Mary's Abbey, 36, 44, 51, 52, 57, 60, 61
St Mary Bishophill Junior, 51
St Mary Castlegate, 51, 115
St Maurice's Road, 91
St Michael-le-Belfry, 53, 64
St Nicholas's Hospital, 52
St Olave's Church, 36, 37, 51
St Paul's Square, 94
St Peter, Church of, 28
St Peter's School, 83, 95
St Sampson's Church, 115
St Sampson's Square, 24, 48, 91, 111
St Saviourgate, 55, 78, 79, 80, 105, 109
St Wilfrid, 29, 80
St Wilfrid's R.C. Church, 95, 96
St William's Chapel, 59, 64, 80
St William's College, 52–54, 57, 83, 97
Salisbury, 48
Scandinavia, 30, 35
Scarborough, 20, 21, 47, 52, 76, 86, 89, 91, 93
Scarborough Castle, 46
Scarborough Road, 103
Scarcroft, 95, 96
Scarcroft Road, 94
School for the Blind, 82, 96
Scotland, 21, 25, 26, 35, 45, 47, 65, 68

Scrope, Lord, 47
Selby, 60, 69, 83, 86
Selby Cut, 75
Septimus Severus, 24, 25
Serapis, 24
Sever, William, 60
Severn, 21
Severus Hill, 98
Shambles, 36, 49, 56, 64, 105
Shaw, Rev. Patrick, 14
Sheffield, Lord, 62
Sheriff Hutton, 76
Sheriff Hutton Castle, 46, 61
Sisters of Charity of St Paul the Apostle, 96
Siward, Earl, 36
Skeldergate, 36, 44, 48, 49, 54, 64, 75, 77, 79, 87, 91, 97
Skeldergate Bridge, 90
Skeldergate Postern, 56, 82, 90
Skelton, 69, 86, 104
Skipton Castle, 46
Solemn League and Covenant, 65
Speed, John, 64, 65
Spofforth Castle, 46
Spurriergate, 77
Stainmore, 21
Stamford Bridge, 38
Stanwick, 21, 22
Star Inn, 78
Station Avenue, 90
Station Hotel, 85, 86
Stephenson, George, 83, 85
Stillington, 55, 76
Stockton, 83
Stonegate, 23, 31, 53, 55, 56, 64, 78, 105, 113
Strensall, 55, 76, 96
Sussex, 30
Swinegate, 48, 91

Tadcaster (Calcaria), 21, 22, 38, 45, 57, 104
Tang Hall, 102, 103, 106
Tanner Row, 35, 84, 85
Tanner's Moat, 88
Tate, Ridsdale, 95

Tempest Anderson Hall, 95
Templenewsam, 70
Terry Avenue, 99
Terry's, 14, 83, 87
Theatre Royal, 95
Thief Lane, 90
Thirsk, 69
Thomlinson Walker's, 87
Thornton, John, 53
Thrush Lane, 91
Thursday Market, 48, 77, 82, 111
Toft Green, 25, 48, 52, 55, 85
Tostig, 38
Tours, 30
Tower Street, 77, 91
Towton, Battle of, 47
Trajan, 22
Treasurer's House, 53, 62, 97
Trent, River, 21, 24, 61, 69
Tuke, Mary, 83
Tuke, William 83
Tuke and Casson, 88
Turpin, Dick, 73
Tyne, River, 39

Unitarian Chapel, St Saviourgate, 80
University of York, 13, 60, 87, 107
Unwin, Raymond, 100

Vanbrugh, Sir John, 70
Venutius, 22
Vermuyden, 69
Vespasian, 22
Via Praetoria, 31, 53, 79, 113
Via Principalis, 31, 37, 44, 52, 65
Vicar's Lane, 53
Victoria, Queen, 85, 86
Victoria Bar, 93
Vikings, 30

Wakefield, 49, 63, 75
Wales, 21, 42
Walmgate, 33, 44, 48, 65, 78, 82, 92, 93, 97, 98,
    102, 105

Walmgate Bar, 44, 45, 65, 82, 92
Walmgate Stray, 55, 96
Walton, George, 95
Wandesforde House, 80
War of the Roses, 47, 48
Water End, 104
Water Lanes, 91, 98
Waterloo Steam Packet, 83
Watling Street, 46
Wearmouth, 29
Welwyn Garden City, 100
Wensleydale, 46
Wentworth, Earl of Strafford, 62, 65
Westminster, 47
Westmorland, 61
West Riding, 64, 69, 94, 97
Wetherby Bridge, 47, 69
Wharfe, 24
Whitby, 25, 29, 47, 51
Widdrington, Sir Thomas, 66
Wiggington Road, 93, 94
Wilkins, William, 95
William the Conqueror, Duke of Normandy, 36,
    38, 39, 41, 47, 88
William of Malmesbury, 45
William Rufus, 51
Windmill Rise, 65
Wintringham, Dr, 79
Women's Prison, 42, 81
Wormald's Cut, 76, 87, 89

York, Duke of, 48
York Aesthetic, The, 108
York and County Bank, 83
York and North Midland Railway Company, 85,
    86
York Archaeological Trust, 17
York Castle, 90, 96
York Civic Trust, 16, 106, 114, 115
York Diocesan Trustees, 97
York Dispensary, 96
York Exhibition, 98
York Footpath Association, 82
York Georgian Society, 14, 16

Index

York Glass Company, 87
York Mercury, 73
York Mystery Plays, 50, 51, 60
York, Newcastle and Berwick Railway, 86
York Savings Bank, 83
York Tramways Company, 101
York Union Bank, 83
York, Vale of, 31, 45, 46, 68

York Waterworks, 74
Yorkshire, 21, 46, 49, 60, 61, 64, 80
Yorkshire Club, 100
Yorkshire Evening Press, 15
Yorkshire Insurance Company, 83, 95
Yorkshire Museum, 90, 95
Yorkshire Savings Bank, 95
Young, Archbishop, 63